Diary

of a

Player

Diary
of a
Player

HOW MY MUSICAL HEROES MADE A
GUITAR MAN OUT OF ME

BRAD PAISLEY

AND DAVID WILD

HOWARD BOOKS
A DIVISION OF SIMON & SCHUSTER, INC.

NEW YORK   NASHVILLE   LONDON
TORONTO   SYDNEY   NEW DELHI

Howard Books
A Division of Simon & Schuster, Inc.
1230 Avenue of the Americas
New York, NY 10020

First Howard Books hardcover edition November 2011

HOWARD and colophon are trademarks of Simon & Schuster, Inc.

For information about special discounts for bulk purchases,
please contact Simon & Schuster Special Sales at
1-866-506-1949 or business@simonandschuster.com

The Simon & Schuster Speakers Bureau can bring authors to your live event. For more information or to book an event, contact the Simon & Schuster Speakers Bureau at 1-866-248-3049 or visit our website at www.simonspeakers.com.

Designed by Jaime Putorti

Manufactured in the United States of America

10   9   8   7   6   5   4   3   2   1

Library of Congress Cataloging-in-Publication Data

Paisley, Brad.
    Diary of a player : how my musical heroes made a guitar man out of me /
Brad Paisley and David Wild. —1st Howard Books hardcover ed.
        p.   cm.
    Includes bibliographical references.
    1. Paisley, Brad.   2. Country musicians—United States—Biography.
    I. Wild, David, 1961–   II. Title.
    ML420.P1445A3 2011
    782.421642092—dc23
        [B]   2011025728
ISBN 978-1-4516-2552-3
ISBN 978-1-4516-2553-0 (ebook)

CONTENTS

BORN ON CHRISTMAS DAY

It's Christmas. I am eight years old. I have just finished opening all of the presents that Santa Claus left under our Christmas tree. Being an only child means that pretty much everything sitting in the general vicinity of that evergreen treasure trove is mine to be plundered. Since I've ripped and pillaged every last wrapped gift, it's time to head to Papaw and Mamaw's. The next step in the ritual of Christmas for the Paisley family is to eat lunch at the grandparents' house and exchange more presents between aunts, uncles, cousins, and in-laws.

As an eight-year-old in 1980, the most important item on my Christmas list was probably plastic, manufactured by Kenner, and said "Star Wars" on the package. In my mind, my life would have had no meaning if something like a Millennium Falcon or a light saber did not appear that Christmas day. I would have had no reason to go on.

As it turns out, I was right about one thing: my life did depend on a gift that I would receive that December 25. But it wasn't any sort of spaceship, laser sword, or action figure.

Sitting beneath a pile of presents under my grandparents' tree was the answer to almost every question that life would ever throw at me, the map I needed to guide me through every twist and turn, a shield that would defend me from heartache, and a battle-axe that would lead me to victory. And one of the best friends I would ever have.

1

WELCOME TO
THE FUTURE

Every day's a revolution . . .

—"Welcome to the Future,"
written by Brad Paisley and Chris DuBois

Warning: this book is *not* an autobiography.

It's more of a look at a life in progress, with strings attached.

I am standing on a stage. In front of me is a sea of people, all very close together, and most of them are staring somewhat hopefully in my general direction. Some are wearing T-shirts and jeans, miniskirts, and tank tops, ball caps, cowboy hats, and camouflage. And other than the people facing the wrong way wearing the yellow vests labeled SECURITY and a few facing the wrong way who are too drunk to know better, this mob is expecting something from me.

As a giant spotlight flashes right on my face, that dramatic glare reminds me of a strange but true fact: all of these people have come here tonight to see Brad Paisley from Glen Dale, West Virginia.

As I stand here basking in the glow of all this, looking out into the darkness at thousands of friends I have never even met, I cannot help but think back to how I got here.

"Here"—I should probably explain—is a curious kind of traveling circus that has my name written all over it. There are roughly two hundred otherwise normal individuals who are all a part of this welcoming and mobile "Village of Paisley." Rather than stay safely in one place like most sane people do, these gypsies crisscross the country together with the help of twelve huge tour buses, as well as the occasional plane, train, and automobile.

The people in our mostly happy and peaceful traveling village spend a big part of their lives on the road living out a shared dream. I'm talking about a dream so big and improbable that I barely could have imagined it growing up. But in fact, I did dare to dream it as a wide-eyed kid living next to a music town in West Virginia. I just didn't dream quite big enough. See, in my mind, the ultimate end-all, be-all ultra-successful music career meant one thing: a bus. Not multiple buses, not lasers, huge LED video walls, tractor trailers, etc.

A bus. Simply put, my dream was to travel our country on a bus with a band and play some songs people knew and loved. I sorta aimed for the moon, shot right by that, and landed in the stars.

So as I stand here tonight in the middle of this dream come extra-true, I can't help but think about everything I have to be grateful for. You could say that music is my life, but a better way to put it is to say music has given me a life. A life with strings attached, usually six at a time. It is how I made my first dime, and therefore bought my first car. It is how I made it through heartaches, challenges, and school. It's how I met my wife. It is how I discovered myself.

I roll the volume up on that shining electric guitar hanging around my neck—the way that I have ten thousand times before—and I start to play. When my hands hit the guitar, something happens that still amazes me. A series of big resounding chords ring out and travel through the night air, making their way from the stage straight into the hearts and minds of the best fans an artist could ask for.

For all of us standing in this wide open space tonight, those guitar chords flying around create a mass vibration that we can all share together but that none of us can ever quite define. Defining it isn't the important thing—*feeling* it is.

That's what brings us all here this evening—that shared need to *feel something*.

And it all goes back to a Christmas gift. A guitar, gift-wrapped and waiting patiently to rock my world. So how did I get from that gift under that fake, plastic bluish-white Christmas tree to some of the largest stages in the world? One guitar hero at a time. And I don't mean the video game.

The foremost guitar hero in my life is a remarkable man who left this world way too soon but who changed my life forever. This man lovingly handed me my first guitar and, in the process, made a real player out of me. I can never fully repay him the debt I owe him for setting me on a brand-new path and introducing me to what would be an incredibly bright future.

When I close my eyes and think back to the earliest memory I can recall, there's one that I can see in my mind as if it were yesterday: I am three or four years old and my two hands are much smaller and have none of the calluses they have now. My toddler self is standing directly in front of my grandfather Warren Jarvis, who is playing away on his beloved Yamaha acoustic guitar.

As my grandfather—or Papaw, as I called him—powers through some bluegrass music, I'm pressing my little hands onto the strings of his guitar—but I'm not trying to play a note. Instead, I am desperately trying to mute the sound and somehow make my grandfather stop playing that weird wooden instrument he loves so much. Papaw sits there for hours at a time playing one country instrumental after another just for his own entertainment, and yet I am using all the strength in my tiny hands to try to make him stop playing guitar so that he will play something else—*anything else*—with me.

I think back to this moment a lot these days because, as fate would have it, I now have two boys who do the exact same thing to me. Just yesterday, my older boy, Huck, walked up to me and requested that I play the theme from *Batman* for him. That sort of request is pretty hard for a dad like me to deny. So I made an E chord and started that immortal semi-annoying melody—*na-na-na-NA* . . . But as soon as I began, Huck pressed his own little hands onto my acoustic guitar strings with all of the veto power of a record executive. "Let's go *play* Batman!" I thought I was doing just that, but obviously my idea of playing Batman is completely different than his.

My grandfather Warren Jarvis—my mother's dad—always picked his guitar while sitting in his favorite chair in the living room of his house. I remember that we always referred to my grandfather's usual place of residence as "the Archie Bunker chair." He had all the ornery irreverence of the TV character. In this case, Papaw's chair was a comfortable old rocker with big wooden arms and a wooden frame and two pillows. My grandfather would always sit on the edge of his seat, holding that Yamaha acoustic guitar in his hands, wearing slippers and slacks—because by law that's precisely the sort of goofy thing a grandfather is supposed to wear. Though he could be one tough customer when he was young, my grandfather had settled into a kind of down-home George Burns by the time I came along and got to know and love him. Sometimes Papaw would even wear a harmonica on a cord around his neck, so that he sort of looked like George Burns meets Woody Guthrie.

For most of the years I was lucky enough to have him in my life, my grandfather worked for the B & O Railroad as a telegrapher and dispatcher, and his shift ran from four P.M. to midnight. I'm not sure now if having that particular shift worked out that well for his sleep patterns, but from my selfish point of view it was perfect. He could spend all day with me before he left around three thirty in the afternoon to head off toward the railroad station.

And most days, that's exactly what he did.

My parents—Doug and Sandy Paisley—both worked day jobs, and I was their only child. My mom was a schoolteacher in town, and my dad was an administrator for the Department of Highways. So instead of day care, surrounded by my own kind, I was off to the wise care of my elders. I was always surrounded by older, wiser people, which would become a recurring theme in my life, for sure.

My grandfather and grandmother always welcomed me, along with my two cousins Lisa and Christy who lived just next door. They offered a safe and loving environment with a well-stocked refrigerator. What more could a kid ask for? Inasmuch as I ever really grew up, I grew up in their little brick house.

So from a very early age I learned the value of the influence of much older people. The bottom line is that I didn't have any brothers or sisters—though I was able to spend a lot of my childhood with two cousins, and had plenty of friends my own age. I was the odd little kid who watched Lawrence Welk and *Hee Haw*; listened to Floyd Cramer records; ate at Mehlman's Cafeteria, where they had an "early-bird senior special"; and could recite from memory the dialogue from Geritol commercials. Oftentimes, I was even dressed by my grandparents, and sadly, my parents have the pictures to prove this—some of which I am loading in our fireplace to burn, and some of which are published here for your entertainment pleasure. You're welcome.

In terms of my approach to life and my overall character, there's no doubt that I am the product of my mother and father. My parents are both good and grounded people who taught me all of life's really big lessons. They are decent, churchgoing, hardworking, great examples. They did the grunt work. The spankings, the groundings, the allowance, etc. They taught me right from wrong, though I still occasionally get the two confused. Grandparents, as a rule though, tend not to be all that big on discipline or administering the especially painful punishments. That's your parents' gig. Grandparents tend to be better at just loving you with an open heart and possibly spoiling you rotten when your parents aren't looking.

So while my parents shaped my character, my grandfather—the man who gave me my first guitar—shaped the course of my life. Without him, I'd be standing on an empty stage. My life would be *completely* different—no hit songs, no sold-out concerts, no website, no merchandise, no tour bus, and absolutely no dedicated fans.

I wish everyone could have known him. Warren Jarvis had a warm smile and a hearty laugh, a smoker's laugh that always eventually ended in a cough. Bald as an eagle, big buck teeth in the front, earlobes the size of large earrings, and never without thick bifocal glasses. He was *the* perfect grandpa. This all somehow made him more human, just the way a few little scratches on a gorgeous guitar make you treasure it even more.

I never knew my grandfather when he was a "young" man. That's just the way of things. In my case, that is definitely best. While he was a warm and charming old goat later in life, he was a real hell-raiser back in the day. I wouldn't have liked that guy, I bet. The story goes that he had to fight very hard to win my grandmother when they were two young people growing up in the same hometown of Huntington, West Virginia. It was the thirties, they were teenagers, and they came from very different backgrounds. My grandmother was a real beauty with dark hair and stunning blue eyes, and so, naturally, this local babe could have had her pick of any of the boys in town. Perhaps as a result of all her excellent options, my mamaw had absolutely *no* interest in dating this Warren Jarvis character.

And so it came to pass that my grandfather took a very interesting, if controversial, approach to overcoming his romantic predicament. Nowadays I believe they call it "stalking." Or maybe "harassment." Basically, he decided to personally intimidate every other single guy in town who tried to date my grandmother. He would follow her to a soda shop or diner on one of her dates and pick a fight with whoever she was with. It would go something like this . . .

> Papaw: *Why you datin' my gal?*
> Chump: *She ain't your gal!*
> Papaw: *We'll see about that.*

Fight.

And . . . here I am.

Unorthodox? Sure. Obnoxious? Yes. Illegal? Well, a few times he got thrown in jail for this behavior, but you really have to hand it to the guy—there was a certain primal brilliance to his logic. Take out the competition. For the record, this is *not* how I eventually won Kim's heart. By that I mean there was no fighting.

I did stalk her.

In my mind, this crazy scene sounds like something right out of a great Loretta Lynn song. With my grandfather as Loretta Lynn. I suppose all is fair in love and war, but my grandfather's approach seemed to bring love and war a little too close for comfort. He wasn't an especially large man, but he knew how to stick up for himself, and he was clearly ready to fight anyone for his dream girl. He had it bad. Beyond bad.

One story that got passed down concerns a time when my grandmother went out on a date with the son of the town's fire chief, and my grandfather knocked this prospective suitor right off his stool in the local drugstore. The police were called, and soon they threw both of these young men in jail for disorderly conduct. They got to share a cell and discuss what had just transpired. Of course, before long the other guy got out of jail because his dad was the fire chief—not to mention he had probably done nothing wrong other than to also have eyes for my smokin' mamaw. I imagine that my grandfather got to serve out the remainder of his jail time pondering just how he was going to *legally* win over my future mamaw's heart.

It was the beginning of World War II. So without much else to lose, Warren Jarvis (now eighteen) went down to the local air force recruitment office and enlisted. He would fight for the air force in the South Pacific for the entire war, in the Philippines and Guam. I imagine that as a soldier it helps to have something else to fight for besides Uncle Sam. I believe he was fighting for Dorothy Douglas, as he'd shown he was all too willing to do. He tirelessly wrote a hundred or so letters to her from over there, even though she was not technically his to write to, and he always let her know what she meant to him. Somewhere, between the time he was gone and when he set foot back in Huntington, she must have actually missed him.

Because not long after he returned, she gave in and got married.

Other than the moment my grandfather somehow won my grandmother's heart, the most important day in the shaping of my future was undoubtedly that Christmas of 1980. As I unwrapped the largest gift under the Jarvis tree, it was clear what Papaw had given me. My grandfather had wrapped up his Sears Silvertone guitar with an amp in the case. That Silvertone guitar was so ugly it was beautiful—all cheesy black sparkles with a little white mixed in.

Truth be told, this may not have been the best first guitar choice for an eight-year-old kid. At the time, that made no difference whatsoever—I quickly plugged it in and tried my little hands at playing it, thrilled to make some kind of noise of my own. My grandfather was especially excited that the amp couldn't get loud enough to hurt my ears—or his—which he proudly pointed out to my parents. They'd be putting up with a lot of racket over the next few years. Or more accurately, the rest of their lives.

That old guitar is probably worth less than $500 today—not a lot by classic guitar standards, but to me it's priceless.

From my perspective, a guitar is the most life-changing machine there is and offers the greatest return on investment you can get. Think about it this way: you can use the cheapest guitar to write the finest song in history. A good song can cost you nothing but a few hours of your time, and it can earn hundreds of thousands of dollars or more. Even the worst broken-down guitar can still give you a career and a very real chance to change the world in some small way.

S O L O

Brad Paisley is a strong part of the future of country music. He is a true superstar, a great stage presence, a dynamic performer, a great singer, and one of the most fantastic guitar players I've ever had the pleasure of picking with. He's not just up there onstage acting this out. He loves to play his music, and the people love

*to hear him play his music. He's a-pickin' and I'm
a-grinnin'.*

—ROY CLARK

More than a quarter century after my grandfather gave
me one of his beloved guitars, I recorded my first largely instrumental album, called *Play*. It's the kind of album I like to
think that Warren Jarvis would have loved. In the liner notes
for that dream project, I paid tribute to the man who made
my dream possible:

*When I was eight I got a gift from my grandpa. No
coincidence that around that time I also got an identity.
See, no matter how I have changed, learned, and evolved
as a person, the guitar has been a major part of it, and
really the only constant. A crutch, a shrink, a friend, love
interest, parachute, flying machine, soapbox, canvas, li-
ability, investment, jackpot, tease, a sage, a gateway, an
addiction, a recovery, a temptress, a church, a voice, veil,
armor, and lifeline. My grandpa knew it could be many of
these things for me, but mostly he just wanted me to never
be alone. He said if I learned to play, anything would be*

manageable, and life would be richer. You can get through some real tough moments with that guitar on your knee. When life gets intense, there are people who drink, who seek counseling, eat, or watch TV, pray, cry, sleep, and so on. I play.

Tonight I will stand on a stage and play a song called "Welcome to the Future" that I wrote with my friend Chris DuBois. It's a song that sees the world through the eyes of someone my age as well as through the eyes of someone older. Sitting there in his cozy slippers and dress pants in that old chair, my papaw looked into a future that he would not live to see himself and helped to make a guitar man out of me. In the process, my grandfather somehow became my very first guitar hero.

Guitar Tips from Brad

LESSON #1

Buy a strap. This is going to be a beautiful, bumpy ride.

2

TIME WELL WASTED

I sure soaked up every minute of the memory we were makin'
And I count it all as time well wasted.

—"Time Well Wasted,"
written by Ashley Gorley and Kelley Lovelace

Considering my current employment situation, I would dearly love to tell you that I took to my chosen instrument like some sort of natural-born guitar hero—a true and instant virtuoso. Unfortunately, that's not quite how things worked in my case. It actually took a little time for me to fully appreciate the gift my grandfather had handed to me.

Sometimes I can be a little slow that way.

I really didn't have much of a chance to say no when it came to playing guitar because, as my grandmother could tell you, my grandfather was clearly not a man who liked to take no for an answer. Even though he wasn't necessarily all that great on the instrument himself, he didn't play to be great; he played for fun. My grandfather's enduring musical passion was for the vivid styles of the greatest country music guitar gods like Chet Atkins and Merle Travis, and that great love of his is in large part why I'm a country guitar player today. Papaw's dream was always to learn this very influential and extremely difficult thumb-picking style in which the player is supposed to keep a bass line going throughout the whole song. I remember Papaw sitting there trying to play songs like "Freight Train" or "Cannonball Rag" but he could never quite figure out their style. So he played them his way. And boy, did he love it.

However he played the guitar, Papaw knew what a gift music was, and that's why he couldn't wait to hand that gift over to me. He couldn't afford very expensive equipment, and he had natural ability, although he was never good enough to take it farther than his own living room; he didn't care. It was one of the purest appreciations for a musical instrument that I will ever see. There was no better way to spend an hour (or four), in his opinion, than picking on that thing. He understood in some instinctive way that playing guitar was the very definition of time well wasted. I also think that something told him that it was my calling.

Maybe someday when I'm older and have spent enough of my time playing and singing for anybody who will listen, I might just give a few of my own guitars away. Like my grandfather before me, maybe I'll hand over a bunch of my axes to someone who can put them to better use while still keep-ing them all in the family. Maybe one or both of my boys will ask to take the old paisley Tele for a spin sometime. Or if my future grandchildren—I hear they're *great* kids, and I can't wait to meet them—show any interest *whatsoever* in making music, I'll probably be ready to hand the keys to my entire guitar stable over to them.

But my two sons are currently just four and two years old, so the chances are pretty good that this peaceful transition of guitar power is a considerable ways off in the future. And for the time being, race cars and superheroes beckon.

That's how I was as a kid too. Like a lot of other things in life, playing guitar is actually kind of fun once you get halfway decent at it, but boy, it sucks at first. Now, as a grown-up, I can barely remember not knowing how to play or even strug-gling to learn the basics. I have gone from awkward beginner to completely at a loss without the instrument around.

It's hard to believe now, but there was a time in my young life when playing guitar *did* seem like a waste of time.

But I was very lucky that my grandfather handed me the gift of making music without pushing it on me in a heavy-handed way. I'm not a great believer in pushing an instrument—or for that matter, much of anything else—too hard on a kid. Besides, I got to do what I wanted in my life. I am not someone who's looking to live vicariously through these little guys. They can be whoever they want to be. I got to do just that. Thank God. And Papaw.

Growing up in my parents' house, I still had enough room to find my own way to music on my own terms. My hardworking parents weren't especially musical. My mother sang in the choir and played a little piano, and my dad had all of the musical ability of a block of granite. Like most of the people of their generation, they enjoyed Bill Haley and His Comets, Chuck Berry, and Glen Campbell, but music was more like something in the background of Mom's and Dad's busy lives than a driving passion.

My papaw, on the other hand, was extremely passionate, maybe even rabid, when it came to music. He was also pretty specific in his tastes—he absolutely *loved* instrumental country music and great vocal country records when the playing and picking were featured prominently. Papaw's absolute favorites were Buck Owens, Chet Atkins, Roy Clark, Merle Haggard, and Johnny Cash—all people I aspire to imitate to this day. It's really quite amazing when I look at how much his tastes rubbed off on me. I am my grandfather's grandson, that's for sure. Thank goodness he wasn't pushing the Captain and Tenille or Tiny Tim. 'Cause if he had, today I would no doubt wear a captain's hat or sing songs about tulips in a strange falsetto.

Along with the free guitar on Christmas morning, my grampa generously offered to spring for a few lessons to get me started. He knew enough to know it's not a very good idea to try to teach your own kid (or grandkid) something like this, so he went down to a local music store and signed me up.

My first guitar teacher was a guy who was probably in his early twenties. Now, this young man shall remain nameless because he was a terrible teacher. And also because I can't remember his name. My only real memory of him now is the way that he would talk on the telephone for the first fifteen minutes or so of my supposed thirty-minute guitar lesson with his girlfriend: "What, snookums? What? No, *you're* perfect . . . no . . . *you* are. No, *you!* Shmoopee, I love you too . . . Mmm-hmm . . . oh well, gotta go, some snot-nosed kid is here for his lesson. I miss you. I miss you more. No, you. You." During the other fifteen minutes of this total waste of money, this goofball would seem distracted and mostly keep asking me something out of the guitar teacher handbook, like, "So, do you have any questions?" Or, "Did you learn what I told you to learn last time?" The answer was usually "Um, not really" or, at best, "Kinda." Then as soon as he could, he would go back to talking on the phone. This guy clearly wasn't the teacher to show me anything. Including how to be debonair.

He did end up having one bright idea—working in a guitar shop, this guy had enough insight into the instrument to tell my grandfather that I probably needed an acoustic guitar to learn on, in addition to that Silvertone electric. I'm sure that was a required sales pitch for music store workers, but still, it was a good idea.

As a result, the time had come for me to get my first acoustic. There was a cheaply made Gremlin acoustic guitar hanging up there in the store, and it was priced accordingly. It was an absolutely horrendous instrument. And who names a product a Gremlin? I guess someone interested in truth in labeling. I can only imagine how much I would have loved a better instrument. The action was too high, and it wouldn't stay in tune. I've heard better sounding guitar *cases*. As bad as it was though, that Gremlin was the very beginning of what would become a lifelong love affair between the acoustic guitar and me.

So here's a suggestion for all the parents of would-be guitar gods out there: Sometimes starting out with a better guitar can seem like a risky investment for a kid, but if you want them to love it, it's got to play well. It's worth the risk to spend a little more money on your little Eddie Van Halen or Bonnie Raitt in training. They may just put you in a nicer nursing home someday if it pays off.

Parents often ask me how old their kids should be before they start playing the guitar. I don't really know. Every kid is different, that's for sure. I'll usually say, "Well, eight years old worked for me," but that's not totally true. I was just buying time on the guitar until I was ten or so and could hear myself getting somewhere. These things take time.

No matter what kind of guitar kids hold in their hands, mastering the guitar is no easy matter for most of us. The unfortunate truth here is that the first things you play on the guitar sound *nothing* like what you are trying to play.

The understandable desire to be an instant pro on the guitar comes across loud and clear on the record I did with my friend Keith Urban called "Start a Band." Written by Dallas Davidson, Ashley Gorley, and Kelley Lovelace, the concept suits us both so well. Keith and I could both instantly relate to a song about that timeless dream of all wannabe rock stars and country stars, going directly from that first guitar lesson to full superstar status, as well as the premise of someone who's never really been all that good at anything else before. I think the two of us were both bitten by the bug early in life and never had a prayer of taking an interest in anything else. Like the song says, "When you're living in a world that you don't understand, find a few good buddies, start a band."

Both Keith and I started out trying to play guitar as little kids—me in my small town in West Virginia and Keith way over on the other side of the world down under in a small town in Australia. And our very different paths led us to the same small city, our li'l hillbilly mecca. As two modern country guitar heroes who frequently collaborate, I am always asked who would win in an all-out duel between the two of us. The answer is obvious: the audience.

I am in awe of Keith's talent; his style and chops are so unique. I think he has more natural ability than anyone I have ever met. He is truly inspiring to watch.

SOLO

I truly believe Brad is from another planet—not sure where, but he is otherworldly gifted. His dexterity, flu-

idity, and precision are extraordinary—and in addi-tion to these shaving techniques, he's also not a bad guitar player. Just for the record, Brad has never actu-ally asked me to start a band, and frankly that hurts!

—KEITH URBAN

There are artists in music who are some equivalent of Super-man or Supergirl. Born stars. I'm a fan of a lot of these artists. People who would be popular and famous almost no matter what they did. Born that way. So absolutely destined for pop-ularity that anyone could see their trajectory. I have never felt like one of those.

I am more like Batman. Flawed, human, lacking that su-perpower that guarantees a career as a superhero. I'll explain. I have talent as a guitar player, for sure . . . but it is not what I would count as considerable or extraordinary. I am better than I probably ought to be, honestly. But I have had to work very, very hard to get to whatever level player I am. And the same would go as a singer or songwriter. I don't think I've ever been what you would call awful, but at the core, I truly feel like I would be at best mediocre if not for ingenuity and sweat. Extreme sweat.

While some people can spit out hit songs like bullets to the chart, or sing like birds as effortlessly as breathing, or take to an instrument like Rain Man to blackjack, that's not me. And I'm not someone who walks into a room and changes the energy, or the life of any party (without being the musical guest). Even the guitar took me years to get proficient enough to enjoy at all, let alone impress anyone else. Then there's singing. Singing is something that accompanies songwriting and playing for me, and while I take it very seriously, my style is not meant to shock or awe. It is meant to convey emotion. And songwriting is something I have sculpted like clay. Thanks to Chris DuBois, the pal I have bounced almost every completed or half-finished fragment idea off of, I feel like I figured out something people want to listen to. But all of these have been a process. And some artists seem to find or write the right songs effortlessly and then ascend to the top of the music world like the space shuttle blasting into orbit, people on a rendezvous with destiny. Meanwhile, I have always felt like an underdog that way, honestly. I'm this weird combination of funny guy/sensitive balladeer who no one knew quite what to make of for a while there. I would see another artist put out a song and fly right by just as my engines were starting to warm up. And then I would have to think my way out of the pigeonhole I was headed into. Whether by making some fancy video to get folks' attention or performing a song that's shocking, impactful, or unique, I feel I have reached superstar status the hard way. It has definitely not been easy. No Kryptonian birthright, no radioactive spider bite. That's right, I'm Batman. I've always liked his story best anyway. He worked for his share of the comic-book universe. I can appreciate that.

Wherever you come from, some truths remain the same. And here's one: all new guitar players desperately want to start out playing "Layla" or "Stairway to Heaven" or "Eruption" right away. We all want to run before we can walk. For most of us, when you're just beginning to play as a kid, you're much more likely to find yourself working on a one-note-at-a-time version of "Twinkle, Twinkle, Little Star" than climbing any stairway to heaven.

But if you have a little patience and you work really hard, then maybe you move on quickly to even greater challenges—like actual songs with maybe a couple of chords. Unless you're a true prodigy, you're going to have to practice for a while being bad before you get any good. And it will seem like a waste of time. I remember that feeling well. But don't worry about wasting time, because it'll be so worth it. It's my experience that in the end, life lessons and guitar lessons begin to blur in all sorts of interesting ways.

A few years ago a smart guy named Malcolm Gladwell wrote a really interesting book called *Outliers: The Story of Success* that takes a serious look at what factors contribute to any individual's success. One of the core conclusions that he reaches in his study is something he calls the "10,000-Hour Rule." Basically, Gladwell writes that no matter what you're doing, you most likely need to spend ten thousand hours working at it before you master it.

> *It's my experience that in the end, life lessons and guitar lessons begin to blur in all sorts of interesting ways.*

Now, I don't know how accurate that figure is for the guitar, but I get the point. Some of you out there reading may have been blessed with the good fortune of being born great at something, but most of us mere mortals still have to get good first, and that process usually takes a little time. I think it was years before I was doing anything you would consider "great." But don't be dismayed. Those weren't bad years. Far from it. They were incredible and exciting in retrospect. A little hobby that seemed like a side interest was gradually becoming my focus. And now here I am.

The big problem here is that getting any young person with a short attention span to spend ten thousand hours doing anything can be an uphill battle. That's never been more true than these days when whatever kids do has to compete with so many attractive options. It can be surfing the Web, playing video games, tweeting, or Facebook. Back in my day, I confess that I played my fair share of Donkey Kong, but even then there was no Web for me to surf and I didn't have a status. Well, yes I did, it just wasn't posted anywhere yet.

Whatever you want to do in this life, I'm here to encourage you not to lose hope or give up during the first hundred or so of those ten thousand hours that it takes to get good. You should know that in my case it took me a while to "get the bug" for guitar, as my grandpa used to call it. He always said it would happen, almost like a slow sickness. And he knew it would take time.

I actually quit playing guitar for one summer because it was just too nice outside and I needed to concentrate fully on playing sports, or at least that's how I pitifully explained it to my grandfather. It's easy to see why I did this—maybe I thought I could get good enough at something like baseball to actually have a future in it. More likely, at nine years old or so, I just felt it was too nice out that summer to stay inside and play the guitar. After all, the guitar is something you primarily just do inside, right? Boy was I wrong. Little did I know how infrequently I would actually play the guitar *inside* in the summer someday. I'd say 90 percent of my gigs from May to September are outside. These days, playing in the summertime is most certainly an outdoor sport. Truth be told, I think what I was really trying to do by taking a break was ease into quitting the instrument altogether. I really just didn't love it yet. It hurt my hands unless I practiced all the time, it didn't sound like anything on the radio, and I was far from good at it. Maybe I wasn't meant to be a player.

After a few months of my premature retirement as a guitarist, my grandfather pulled me aside one day and asked me, "So, Brad, you still playing guitar?" I reminded Papaw that I had stopped for the summer. I could see that this news just broke his heart, though he tried to hide it. Here this man had given me one of his prized guitars to play and I was just slacking off and making excuses. My grandfather looked at me sadly and let it go for a little while. Then one day, he said some words that have stayed with me always: "Brad, I sure wish you'd try that guitar again because I'm telling you right now—you're really gonna need it when you get older." Papaw was more right than even he could have known.

After summer, for some reason I decided to pick the guitar back up—and that instantly made my grandfather happy. Soon I started figuring out a thing or two and was able to play what sounded like actual songs. I had reached a crucial point in any player's progress. I had learned exactly enough on the guitar to impress myself and maybe a few other people. I was still a little too young to care about impressing girls with my guitar prowess, but don't worry, I eventually got there too.

I think back to so many nights when my mother—a wonderful teacher no less—was understandably distraught concerning my lousy study habits. I like to think that I was a pretty smart guy before and after the school bell rang, but in between, I was no straight-A student. Part of my problem was that I was able to pass most classes without ever opening a book. I was exactly smart enough to get a B or C without really trying. But being a mediocre student is a bit of a problem when your mom is not only a teacher at your school but one of your teachers too. In her mind, without good grades I would never amount to anything. In my mind, I had a plan that bypassed school completely. And I had no idea how much of a long shot it was. I remembered hearing about how Steve Wariner had left school at seventeen to go on the road with Dottie West. I figured there had to be some tour bus out there with an empty bunk that needed my services.

So much time was spent arguing about my academics with my parents, who thankfully cared a lot about me and how I was doing. All these years later, research has shown that playing music can enhance a person's other academic studies, math especially. But it doesn't take into account the temptation to quit school altogether and go for the big time. That certainly can't help your math scores.

Back then, I really just wanted to play, and studying stayed on my back burner. Not only that, it got in the way. On some level, I just knew I had a musical destiny. And in my case, it just so happens that I turned out to be right when I told my parents that listening to music had to come before listening to lectures in class. I'm not suggesting that any kids out there try that at home—or at school for that matter. But in my case, a little tunnel vision actually worked out quite well. One thing I've learned is that everybody's path in life is a little different, and sometimes the road less traveled pays off.

I was in third grade and a member of the Glen Dale Methodist Church children's choir when they asked me to learn a few songs on the guitar. They thought it would be cute for a kid to back them up, as opposed to the usual little old lady on piano.

They gave me the music for "Try a Little Kindness"—the great Glen Campbell song—and "Life's Railway to Heaven" to play for the kids. So when I went in to discuss playing at the Sunday service, the choir director asked if I knew them well enough yet. I'd been working on them at home, so I started playing and singing right then and there. The choir director must have been at least a bit impressed and said, "Forget about us—*you* sing and play it this week." So dressed in my Sunday best, which was more than likely pleated pants, penny loafers, and a sweater vest . . .

I played.

People clapped.

And the rest is history.

If anyone thought I was great, it was probably because I had the major (if fleeting) advantage of being nine. When you're young, if you're any good at anything, people tend to think you're great. It's all relative.

That Sunday, in front of forty-seven people at the early service and another seventy-six at the late, my whole performing life began.

Back then in Glen Dale, we didn't need the social media like Twitter or Facebook to create buzz. We had churchgoers. Someone at church that day came up and said, "Well, if Brad knows a couple more songs, we could have him play at the church picnic next month."

> *If anyone thought I was great, it was probably because I had the major (if fleeting) advantage of being nine.*

By then my guitar teacher had become a man named Clarence "Hank" Goddard. So he put together a little band specifically for the church picnic. It was at this picnic that we would be offered our first big pay date: one hundred dollars to play the Fireman's Christmas Party. That's right. The big time. And this same little band would become my music school, my vehicle, and my focus for the next several years. And Hank Goddard would become the second-most important guitar player I would ever know.

Guitar Tips from Brad

LESSON #2

Practice makes perfect—or at the very least, practice makes you a little less lousy.

3

MORE THAN JUST THIS SONG

I met this angel with callused hands who let this boy into his band
Under his wing, I learned to fly on these six strings through this life

—"More Than Just This Song,"
written by Brad Paisley and Steve Wariner

My second guitar hero was one of the finest people I will ever know—Clarence "Hank" Goddard. Hank, as everybody called him, came into my life after one traumatic night when my grandfather realized that to get me where I was going musically, he was going to need some professional help.

My parents still remember coming home that evening when my grandparents—who also doubled as my lead babysitters—were watching me while they went out. They came in the front door just as I was rushing upstairs to bed, in tears. My folks came after me, asking what on earth had happened. I told them, "Papaw and I had a fight," and said that I didn't want to talk about it. My father came into my bedroom a little later, but all that he could get out of me was that I had a big argument with my grandfather.

In any family, you're going to have the occasional disagreement, if not a whole bunch of them. So my father decided to let the whole matter go for the time being while I cooled down. Then a couple of minutes later, the phone rang. It was my grandfather calling, sounding *very* serious. "Can I talk to Brad, please?"

My dad grew even more concerned and baffled by what had gone down and asked my grandfather what the heck was going on. "Just let me talk to Brad," he replied. So Dad backed off and handed me the phone. A few moments later, after hearing nothing, Dad heard me say, "That's okay, Papaw."

Warren Jarvis—a man with a big heart, a hot head, and a great deal of pride—had called to apologize to me.

Just like that, our fleeting family crisis was over, and I handed the telephone back to my dad. Only then did Papaw come clean to my father about the multigenerational musical skirmish that had just taken place.

Warren Jarvis—a man with a big heart, a hot head, and a great deal of pride—had called to apologize to me.

"I practiced this guitar piece for two weeks to show Brad something," my grandfather told my dad. "He wouldn't listen; he kept acting like he knew more than I did," he said, clearly upset at my lack of respect. He summed it up:

"Then Brad picked up the guitar and said, 'No, that's not how it's done. *This* is how it's done.' And he played it so much better than me."

I was comfortable enough around him to be a bit of a show-off. After telling this to my father, my grandfather paused a moment, as if to consider the implications of what had just gone down. Then he said with all seriousness, "Doug, we better get Brad some real lessons. The boy's better than me now."

Warren Jarvis really was a proud man, but his love and concern for me were much bigger than a little bruised pride. And so he decided that if I was going to have a real guitar teacher, then I ought to have the very best. I suppose he also figured that if I was really going to pass him by on the guitar, I might as well lap him too. So I didn't just need a guitar teacher. I needed *the* guitar teacher. And in our little world in West Virginia, there was simply no guitar player better in my grandpa's eyes than Hank Goddard.

Clarence "Hank" Goddard was so much more than just your local garden-variety guitar god—he was a regional legend with obvious world-class talent. Long before I met him, he'd already mastered his instrument and seen the world while playing with one of those great USO bands during the Korean War. This man was so incredibly fluent and expressive on the guitar that he could have gone anywhere and played with anyone on any given night. Clarence could play anything you requested by his own guitar heroes, like Les Paul, Chet Atkins, or Merle Travis.

Clarence was nicknamed "Hank" after Hank Garland, a famously gifted Nashville cat who played on countless classic recordings by Elvis Presley, Patsy Cline, and Roy Orbison. In all my years of touring and meeting some of the best instrumentalists the world has ever known, I can honestly say now that Hank Goddard was in the same class as any of them and better than most. But after serving in the Korean War, Hank Goddard came home and chose small-town living over the big time. Hank wanted to stay close to home and to his family, even though his extraordinary talent could have taken him to countless stages across the country. He would live out his days in quiet obscurity in the little town of Moundsville, West Virginia. But with the way Warren Jarvis saw it, I was raised thinking this man was one of the most successful guitarists in the entire world, a household name, an icon, someone everyone knew, a legend. I remember shaking his hand at church when I first met him and running home and telling Papaw, "I met him! I actually met him! And I think I saw the calluses on his hands!" As if Eric Clapton had gone to our church and said hello to me one Sunday.

By the time my grandfather came to the savvy and nervy conclusion that the great Hank Goddard was the one and only man to teach his grandson how to play guitar and turn him into a real player, Hank Goddard had already decided that he was pretty much done with making music for a living, and especially with teaching guitar to difficult little kids. He'd had some previous frustrating experiences trying to teach young people and had sworn off this tedious work for good.

Still, my grandfather was convinced he knew what was best, and he enlisted his son-in-law to make it happen by whatever means necessary. When my father approached Hank—one of the nicest men who you could ever meet—about teaching me, he turned us down politely but flatly, saying, "Doug, I appreciate your faith in my abilities, but I really don't have any interest in teaching right now."

As we all knew by now, my grandfather had never been one to take no for an answer, even if it meant a few hours in lockup. Based on his experiences with a far more stubborn young woman, the man had good reason to believe that he could get whatever he really wanted. So, true to form, Papaw kept pushing my parents and convincing them that they *had* to make this happen for me.

Finally, Hank's resolve to permanently avoid this punk Paisley kid started to weaken. Hank made a concession. He told my father that his daughter Denise could play guitar well enough to teach a little kid like me, and maybe I could come over if we wanted to try that. And every now and then he would stop by and see how I was doing. And maybe, just maybe, when I got to a level where I needed a little more than just book learning on the instrument, he'd sit down and show me a few things.

We jumped at the opportunity to get our foot in the Goddard family home, so my dad started bringing me down to their house after school on Tuesdays for a thirty-minute guitar lesson. The first time, my father went off on an errand in town and came right back. Well, it didn't take too long before my dad realized that he didn't need to come back for at least an hour or so, if he didn't just want to wait around. After Hank's daughter would give me a lesson, Hank himself would casually wander by, take a quick listen, and then sit down and start working with me himself.

Here's how my dad remembers things from those days: "Suddenly, it would be around eight o'clock at night, and I would be trying to get Brad home to do his homework. Meanwhile, Hank's wife is trying to run Brad off because it's getting late. But even with the clock ticking, you just couldn't break those two up when they started jamming."

Having a guitar teacher like Hank Goddard would have been more than enough good fortune for any young player in the world. Yet somehow my luck didn't stop there. Almost right away, Hank Goddard became not just my greatest guitar teacher and my musical mentor but my bandleader.

And it all began at that church picnic. I was asked to play a few songs after the way I rocked the house of God with that first performance. By this time, Hank and I were getting to be fast friends, so I'm sure just to be nice, Hank said, "I'll tell you what, I'll get Gene Elliott to get his drums back out. We can put a little band together for this picnic." Gene was a man in his fifties then who hadn't played in a while. "And maybe Dick Ward will dust off his old guitar and Tom Berisford can bring his bass, and I'll play too." So suddenly I'm playing the big church picnic with not only my guitar teacher but also these other veteran musicians—a band of brothers, or rather, a band of grandpas.

We learned ten songs for the church picnic—at least I did, because all these older guys already knew every song in the book, and a few that never made it to the book too. Right from the start, I was just this young whippersnapper trying his best to keep up with these guys. I would sing simple country songs, and Hank would play these ridiculously complicated jazzy instrumentals, like "Cherokee" or "Birth of the Blues."

Hank taught me by example, and that was true onstage and off. Despite his obvious talent as a musician, Hank was the kindest man imaginable. I look back at old videotapes of me playing in the band with Hank, and I still can't believe that he and the guys put up with me. By that time I was playing a cheap Hondo Strat copy—yet another in a series of terrible guitars that I played in the beginning. As much as I would have loved something like an actual Fender or Gibson, we just weren't made of money. Finally, I got a Tokai Strat, and that was as close to the real thing as it got for me in 1985. I didn't get my first actual Fender until high school, I think.

Suddenly I'm playing the big church picnic with not only my guitar teacher but also these other veteran musicians—a band of brothers, or rather, a band of grandpas.

Whatever I was playing, I'll never forget what it felt like

to have a master like Hank look at me onstage and say en-thusiastically, "Take it, Brad!" In my mind, those are the mo-ments in time when music became a wide-open canvas for me—a place where I could at least try to express something unscripted on the fretboard. Not that I could take any song all that far out. But I'd plink around on something jazzy like "Cannonball Rag" or maybe "Freight Train," and then Hank would save me by taking it right back and playing something absolutely brilliant. Every time I took a solo, I was well aware that Hank was always standing there cheering me on, hoot-ing and hollering as if I was the second coming of Joe Pass. I'd be struggling through an improvised part of a solo and hear, "There you go! That's the way!" from the other side of the stage. What a selfless, giving man. I honestly don't think that I have it in me to do what Hank did for me—stand there night after night with a big, generous smile on his face while some little ten-year-old hotshot in Reebok tennis shoes abso-lutely *murders* "Dill Pickle Rag." Hank was a much better man than me in so many ways, and that's just one. Looking back, though, that's when I started to become a professional musi-cian. I was learning to solo. Or to "Take it, Brad!"

So how exactly did a ten-year-old amateur like me end up working for years with a bunch of middle-aged professionals?

Like a lot of things in my life, the truth is that it just worked out that way.

That is the amazing thing about my little West Virginia success story—I never really had to ask to play because people kept asking me. The very same guy who booked that first church picnic also needed a band for a luncheon months later at the Delf Norona Museum in Moundsville, West Virginia. And before that, the Fireman's Christmas Party called and offered us a hundred dollars plus free beer for the band, and milk for the star. So we took the gig, and we decided to call ourselves Brad Paisley and the C-Notes because it seemed to us like just about everybody who booked us wanted to pay us a hundred dollars to play. From there, it snowballed into steady weekends at every little event you can imagine. There I was fourteen years old, and the guys in the band were close to sixty. By the time I was in junior high school, my friends started to jokingly refer to me and my modernly mature band members as "Brad Paisley and the Seniles."

You might be wondering why a bunch of accomplished musical veterans would tolerate backing up someone too young to get a driver's license. Well, these guys were really doing this for one reason, and that was to give me this opportunity. They believed in me. They all had children of their own and a soft spot in their hearts for a kid with this much passion for music. It also was fun. I mean, we really had more work than we could handle there for a while.

Come on, what Lions Club or Knights of Columbus dinner on earth would *not* want to brag about *that* booking? A preteen with his band of card-carrying AARP members? I may not have been all that hot of a guitar player yet, but nobody else knew that. And thanks to my youth and charm, I was, at the very least, public relations gold.

Think about it this way. Say you're running a nice local family event in West Virginia and you have a choice: You could book a really in-demand, hip local rock band with all the baggage they carry. *Or* you could get the C-Notes, complete with a nifty twelve-year-old front man and a sweet old-timer rhythm section. It wasn't even close to a fair fight, and that's why we won so often. Hank and all the guys in the C-Notes had tremendous skill and seasoning on their side, and I had my youth. Add it up, and we were getting all the gigs we could handle—and gradually earning more than a hundred dollars here and there.

People have heard about Brad Paisley and the C-Notes over the years and asked me what it was like being a kid playing with a bunch of old guys. It's yet another example of the way I seem to bond with older generations. And I realized through this experience how much you can learn watching true veterans do what they do. Not to mention how these guys lived their lives. They were all humble, fun-loving, supportive people who were great role models for me. I will never be able to fully repay them for the lessons I learned by their side.

My time with the C-Notes ruined me in one lasting way—after playing with them, I've never had any tolerance for destructive behavior in my bands. I don't need a musician cultivating his drug habit or trying to live out that whole escape-on-the-road fantasy on my dime. So many musicians turn to the road life as a place to escape from reality and leave the rules of decent society in the dust behind the tires of their buses. Frankly, the appeal of that whole myth has never made much sense to me. As someone who's been lucky enough to get paid to make music most of my life, I don't think there's much to escape from. Of all possible professions on earth, why would you ever need to escape from *this*? To pretend music at this level is a hard life? Come on, on our *hardest* day, we're basically on vacation, and I think we should remember that. Why in the world do you have to unwind so badly from a job that's called *playing*?

Whether he was playing guitar or just talking to me in between sets, I loved listening to Hank Goddard. Hank had a lifetime of stories and knowledge to share with me, and I was happy to soak them up along with all the guitar lessons. Hank told me about how he enlisted in the army and they sent him around the world with a guitar—a nice fifties Telecaster. When he came back home from the war, Hank got a day job at the Triangle Wire and Pipe Plant in Moundsville, West Virginia, and played music on the weekends. He was a spectacled, clean-cut man with a warm smile, soft-spoken demeanor, and incredible sense of humor. He loved his normalcy in small-town USA. He and his wife, Eileen, raised a daughter, Denise, who as I mentioned was briefly my teacher as well. Just

Why in the world do you have to unwind so badly from a job that's called playing?

when Hank thought he was out of the music business, a ten-year-old who worshipped him dragged him back in kicking and screaming. For whatever reasons, Hank decided to play a little longer with me, and for me. No matter what other honors I have or may receive in this world, there's one I will always treasure: Hank Goddard shared his time, talent, and generosity of spirit with me—an inexperienced little kid—and almost single-handedly taught me how to be in a band.

Over the years, people would go up to Hank and say, "You could have been so big. You could have played the Grand Ole Opry and everything. Why did you walk away from all that?" Hearing that question again and again could not have been easy. In the end, I think the bottom line was that Hank Goddard simply didn't want "all that" bad enough. He had heard one too many stories about people whose lives were ruined by the big time, and he erred on the side of caution in gracefully deciding to settle down in Moundsville, West Virginia. I think he was too well-adjusted to do whatever it took to make it as a musician. Hank always used to tell me, "Brad, I just didn't want to live out of a suitcase. I am going to enjoy seeing you take on the world though. You go get 'em."

So I did.

A month before I was supposed to leave for Nashville, Hank Goddard walked out on his back deck after lunch on a Sunday, and a neighbor saw him fall lifeless to the ground. He was a deep shade of blue. His neighbor was a registered nurse who immediately started CPR. My dad, an EMT, heard the call and met the ambulance at the ER. After three attempts with the paddles, his heart restarted. When I heard what had happened, I took off running from my house up the road toward the hospital, which wasn't too far. When I got there, they told me Hank was stable, but his heart had stopped for several minutes. The question would be whether or not he had brain damage. When Hank Goddard came to, I'm told one of the first things he asked was, "Doc, after all this, will I be able to play the piano?" To which the doctor replied, "Most certainly!" Hank said, "Great! 'Cause I couldn't do that before."

Hank had multiple bypass surgeries, and I'm so happy to know that he lived to see me drive out of town and eventually got to read about himself in *Guitar Player* magazine. I've raved about his talent in just about every guitar publication that has ever interviewed me. The truth is that Hank Goddard deserves to be in all the guitar rags based on his monumental ability alone, and whenever I could help him get in one, that meant the world to me.

One of the first things I bought with the first royalty check I ever received was a Gibson Chet Atkins hollow-body electric. But it wasn't for me. I drove home that Thanksgiving and walked right up onto Hank's porch and handed it to him. I said, "This doesn't even begin to pay you back, but here you go. I owe you everything." I think that's the only time I really ever saw him cry.

In March of 2008, while I was working on my guitar-heavy *Play* album, I got a very bad case of the flu and had a 102-degree temperature. I must have slept for three days. Then in the middle of this strange fevered state, I had a melody in my head and an idea for a song about Hank. Lying in bed and burning up, I came up with some of the words for the first verse: "I met this angel with callused hands who let this boy into his band . . ." I remember typing those words into my computer and immediately falling right back into some fever dream. The next morning, I woke up and found out that my friend and teacher Hank Goddard had passed away that night just as I was writing about him. He had been battling cancer. This was such a strange moment of serendipity that at first I just couldn't get over it.

After Hank Goddard died, I felt it was important that he be properly honored in the community where he spent so much of his life. And so I wrote a personal tribute to him in our local paper in West Virginia.

MY MENTOR, THE MASTER

As barges go up and down our mighty Ohio River they leave a tremendous wake. I think some lives are like that. One person in particular passed away last week that changed my life, and the Ohio Valley deserves to know more about him. His name was Clarence Goddard, his friends knew him as "Hank."

As a kid, my grandfather would tell me stories about this local legend, this guitar player named Hank Goddard who was every bit as good as anyone who ever held a pick.

He worshiped Hank's talent and taught me to as well. I was not aware until later that the rest of the world didn't know who Hank was. I was brought up to think he was as famous as they get. I remember going to a weekend backyard party at Mayor Biggie Byard's house in Glen Dale. Hank was playing lead guitar and my Papaw took me over to him to watch and learn. I couldn't believe this international superstar was this close. I figured he must be on a break from touring the country and just playing here on a day off. When he heard this 8-year-old who wanted to learn guitar was there, Hank turned his back to the band and basically gave me a lesson as they played.

This was the first of many.

At 11 years old I was invited to play at the church picnic and Hank put together a small band for me, which went on to play at Glen Dale Fire Department parties, church events, clubs, VFW's, nursing homes, political rallies, fairs, infinity and beyond. We were called the C-Notes. Some of you may remember us, a 12-year-old front man with three AARP members backing him up, Gene Elliott, Tom Berisford and Hank, a semi-retired world class lead guitarist who had played in the military, in Europe and with countless jazz and country bands over the years, and then in mine. I look back now at my luck and I can't believe it.

Here was a man who was willing to take a kid under his wing, all the while standing in the background. He was incredible, he could play ANYTHING from Chet to Les Paul, Hank Garland to Joe Pass; and yet if you look back at those videotapes, there I am with my cheap

Japanese Strat, flogging away and playing way out of tune with him grinning ear to ear. No ego about it. A master guitarist, standing in the shadows, letting an unpolished little upstart take the lead.

When someone would gush about his talents, he would blush and say they were too kind.

When we were paid well for a gig, he would come over to my dad and say, "Let Brad have most of it. He's the front man." He insisted I take a solo in every song, right next to him. He would hold back and make sure I never looked out of my league. He was humble and selfless. He taught me how to lead a band and he treated everyone with respect and kindness.

He led his family in the same gentle way. He was an incredible father, husband, grandfather, worker, and friend. I learned so much from him, from how to treat people to how to handle praise. And so I have spent the bulk of my career trying to honor him. I talk about him in interviews; I mention with pride the way I was taught by a master. And I wanted to write this today because I feel so strongly that his talent was extraordinary. I want my hometown to feel pride in his life and the overabundance of talent we are so blessed to have in this area.

It's not right that he passes on silently without recognition. If you know who I am, if you have enjoyed my songs on the radio, if you've ever wondered how I got to this level, well, one person is at the top of the list of who's responsible. His name was Clarence "Hank" Goddard. He left a wake the size of a river barge. I will spend all my days trying to live up to the example he set for me, with this career that he made possible for me.

I thank God for Hank Goddard.

Days later, I called Steve Wariner. Besides having charted more than fifty singles on the country charts, including ten number one smashes, like "Holes in the Floor of Heaven," "Some Fools Never Learn," and "You Can Dream of Me," Steve was another big influence on me as a guitar player, and a very close friend. In addition to our love of music, Steve and I had something else in common: we each had a brilliant guitar teacher who had meant the world to us. The man who took Steve under his wing was none other than the great Chet Atkins—who was himself perhaps the ultimate guitar hero to my grandfather, Hank Goddard, and pretty much the world.

Because I knew that Chet Atkins was like a father to Steve, I asked Steve to come over, and I shared the song I had begun to write. "You wanna write your own verses of this song for Chet?" I asked him. One of my more treasured possessions is a photo of Chet, Hank, and me. Though I had the honor of meeting Chet on a few occasions, I didn't get to know him personally, but I feel like I knew him through Steve, who has shared a million Chet stories with me over the years.

Chester Burton Atkins—better known as Chet—was one of the most respected and influential figures in the history of country music and American music generally. He was born dirt-poor in the tiny Appalachian town of Luttrell, Tennessee, yet somehow he became a symbol for sophistication in country music. Chet became known as "Mr. Guitar," and you don't need me to point out that the man picked as well as anyone ever has.

One of my more treasured possessions is a photo of Chet, Hank, and me.

You can still hear Chet's extraordinary playing on countless recordings, including songs by Hank Williams, Kitty Wells, Elvis Presley, and the Everly Brothers. Next time you hear "Cold, Cold Heart" by Hank Williams or "Heartbreak

Hotel" by Elvis, think for a moment about the great Chet Atkins standing right beside them playing his guitar. And when you hear one of those incredible Everly Brothers classics like "Wake Up Little Susie" or "Bye Bye Love," reflect on the fact that the Everlys might not have made nearly as much musical history if Chet Atkins hadn't been not only in the studio with them, but also in their corner.

Chet Atkins was much more than a great player. His trademark "Atkins style," which my grandfather and Hank Goddard loved, is very hard to master. Of course, Chet was influenced by hearing Merle Travis before him, as well as other all-time guitar greats, like Django Reinhardt and Les Paul. As the story goes, Chet heard Merle on some old-time radio program, playing with his thumb and index finger on his right hand, and just assumed Merle had to be using at least three fingers.

That's how Chet developed his own distinctive style of playing with his thumb and the first two fingers on his right hand—occasionally the first three. That's the same style that countless others have tried to master, most of them failing miserably. That's also the style my grandfather loved and the style that somehow came easy to Hank Goddard. Thanks to

Hank, it's a style that I learned and that is part of the bedrock of how I play today.

More than anyone, Chet built what became known as the Nashville Sound. When Chet was running RCA Records' country division, he helped bring the world a generation of great artists, including legends like Waylon Jennings, Dolly Parton, Jerry Reed, and Charley Pride. Before he passed in 2001, Chet Atkins did it all, and he did it all well. Chet once said, "Years from now, after I'm gone, someone will listen to what I've done and know I was here. They may not know or care who I was, but they'll hear my guitar speaking for me."

I think it's safe to say that Chet Atkins's guitar is still speaking to us and speaking very eloquently.

Steve Wariner and I spoke about our two amazing guitar teachers, and soon we finished the song that we wrote together for Hank and Chet—two guys to whom we owed "more than just this song." When it came time to record it, I brought Hank's personal guitar from back in West Virginia to the session. Steve brought one of Chet's guitars. In the studio, when I opened up the case of Hank's old Gibson to show Steve, we found the bulletin for Hank's funeral laying right there on top. A second later Steve opened up the case that held Chet's guitar, and right on the top was the bulletin for Chet's memorial service at the Ryman. Looking almost identical! It turns out Steve had used the guitar when he played Chet's service and hadn't taken it out. Steve and I both felt like we were in some strange *Twilight Zone* episode. When the song was finished, I felt such a sense of pride. It really did capture who they were, I think, and I know that Hank would have loved being remembered right there alongside Chet Atkins, right on top where he *always* belonged.

Thank you, Hank, for all those years of telling me, "Take it, Brad." From the bottom of my heart, I don't think that I ever would have taken it nearly as far without you and your shining example.

Guitar Tips from Brad
LESSON #3

Start off acoustic. You have a lifetime to get plugged in.

4

CELEBRITY

When you're a celebrity
It's adios reality

—"Celebrity,"
written by Brad Paisley

So I got pretty good on the guitar. And now people know who I am. Good-bye anonymity.

As the song "Celebrity" suggests, sometimes saying hello to celebrity means saying adios to reality. Almost monthly, someone out there reinvents what it means to lose touch due to fame.

Some of you probably remember the video we did for "Celebrity," costarring my friends William Shatner and Jason Alexander. The video made fun of what modern celebrity looks and sounds like here in the twenty-first century. Looking back at the video recently, I couldn't help but notice that all three of us goofing around in the video were anything but overnight success stories. Here's what you might not know: before William Shatner went off on any star trek, entering that dangerous stratosphere of fame and fortune, he paid his dues and studied hard to become a trained Shakespearean actor back home in Canada.

By the same token, way before Jason Alexander became George Costanza on *Seinfeld,* he first became a major theatrical sensation onstage in New Jersey and later a Tony-winning actor on Broadway. It's important to take plenty of time to get good at something substantive before you focus on getting famous. This just makes good common sense to me. And it's true whether you're playing a guitar, acting, or working behind the scenes.

But in our culture today, the paradigm has shifted. It's a very different process, this fame-and-fortune game. In the earliest days of pop culture, people did something well and then became successful and known. The horse was properly in front of the cart. The horse being unique ability, the cart being fame and fortune. Now it's almost always cart first, horse optional.

> *It's important to take plenty of time to get good at something substantive before you focus on getting famous.*

That's why I relate to guitar players. There is no way to cheat at being skilled in this field. If you are known for your sound, for your style, your unique ability, then you got there woodshedding. Almost no other way around it. Unless you went down to the crossroads, sold your soul to the devil, and made that deal. But that's only happened once, I'm told.

As a famous person, I look for inspiration in people who have earned their status.

One of the most talented and successful people I have ever known is my pal John Lasseter, the groundbreaking and visionary animator, writer, director, and chief creative officer of Pixar who's behind the *Toy Story* franchise and some of the greatest films of our lifetime. But before John ever ran Pixar and became the principal creative adviser for Walt Disney Imagineering in his spare time, he was a creative little kid drawing cartoons during church services in Whittier, California. Long before he ever became an animator at Disney, John got his first experience with the company as a Jungle Cruise skipper at Disneyland in Anaheim, and my guess is that John was as good as any tour guide they ever had at Disneyland. He is someone who always does his best at anything he does and always will. If you want to be a successful guitar player, be that in a guitarist.

When people ask me for advice about "making it" in music today, the first thing I usually tell them is that they should try to make it—meaning music—in their own backyard first, before they start worrying about the big time. I could be wrong, but "deciding" to be a star and then rushing off to Nashville or Hollywood or New York seems just a little silly and potentially dangerous. It's the easiest way to get that horse-and-cart thing all askew.

There are lots of advantages to trying to be a hometown hero before you rush out and try to conquer the rest of a watching world. First of all, ask Genghis Khan or Alexander the Great: it's a lot easier to conquer a small town than a whole country. Okay, bad example. But starting out taking things a little smaller and slower gives you the time and space to actually get good *before* you get famous. Go rack up some of those first ten thousand hours you need in front of friends and family, before hitting the world stage. They will love you and protect you. That's a good thing too. In this day and age of YouTube and TMZ, if you aren't already great when you get everyone's attention, there will be plenty of proof out there. Especially if you're thinking about enjoying a life in music, as opposed to just grabbing your fifteen minutes of fame. Practice now, young pickers. You won't have time later. After all, it's a little like the dog that tries to catch the car. What do you do with it once you've actually caught it?

Then there is the fortune that accompanies the fame.

I've always said that I'm grossly overpaid for what I do. In this world there are people in professions that save lives, save countries, and even to some extent the planet, and yet they may never reach my income level. I'm by no means Bill Gates, but it is a strange feeling to have more than enough money at most times. It is something I struggle with, in that there can be a guilty feeling, especially when you meet people in need. It is probably obvious that I have a soft spot for Corvettes and fast cars, even more obvious that I like guitar gear . . . and, therefore, own more than my fair share of each.

My way of justifying this type of extravagance has always been to give back. I try my best to make sure I offset this opulence as best I can. Randy Owen from Alabama was a great example to me in this way. He was chiefly responsible for getting country radio involved with St. Jude Children's Hospital. One year at the Country Radio Seminar, he stood up, made a presentation, and dared everyone in the country music community to do something for this cause. It worked. All these years later, Country Cares has raised hundreds of millions of dollars for that children's hospital. Early on in my career I met Randy at a St. Jude event, and he approached me about that very subject. He said, "Brother Brad, when you look back on your career, I'm here to tell you what will matter. It won't be gold records or awards. It will be this [*pointing at the kids assembled in the room*]. It'll be what you did with it to make lives better that matters." I never forgot that. And so while I miss the mark sometimes in that area, I'm always happiest when I am making up for my spoils.

Today's world of reality shows and televised talent shows is certainly new. Everyone wants to be rich and famous. I understand the wealth side of these desires. On the other hand, I'm a little less clear on our culture's intense and slightly scary obsession with fame. I confess that I sometimes find it hard to relate to the young musicians I meet who have this overwhelming hunger and fire to move to Nashville just to get a record deal right away. It's always obvious to me when someone is making music for the fame, rather than achieving fame due to the music. I saw a great deal of that sort of raw ambition when I studied at Belmont University in Nashville.

From what I saw then and since, too many of these kids get overly aggressive and actually blow some chances by being too pushy. Some of these ambitious young people I've met in Nashville remind me a little of Rachel Berry on *Glee*, the character played by Lea Michele—you know, the type who's always a little too willing to tell you absolutely *everything* she knows. And in that way, you start to realize how little she actually knows. Mark Twain said, "It is better to keep your mouth closed and let people think you are a fool than to open it and remove all doubt."

Growing up where I did, around people like my family and Hank Goddard and the guys in the C-Notes, I learned a very different sort of show business reality. All of the influences I was lucky to meet along the way showed me that you could come at a life in music from a different approach—that maybe it's better to start out being timid and sitting back a bit, waiting in the wings and learning a few things while you are there. In a nutshell, practice. Watch and learn for a while. I certainly don't like the feeling of looking like a fool any more than the next guy.

I remember competing in exactly one talent show— definitely *non*-televised—and I didn't much like the experience (and not just because I didn't win). Somehow it just felt wrong to me, because as I've come to understand it, making music isn't about competition. It's about collaboration. *I am a player.* And I play *with* people, not against them. Guitar playing is not a race or a popularity contest by nature.

I also auditioned as a performer exactly once in my life, and it was for Opryland. While most of it went very well— they loved my guitar playing and really were interested in me as a singer—there was also a dance portion that was *not* optional. So yours truly had to perform some sort of dance routine for the judges, complete with freestyle section and everything. My college adviser Jim "Coach" Watson went with me that day and is the only person alive who witnessed this absolute disaster, other than the judges. The request was, "Show us you can dance."

I moonwalked.

That's right. Yeah, baby. That was my freestyle dance routine. I moonwalked. In 1992. Ten years late, actually. And in full view of Nashville judges. Needless to say, I realized that day that the audition process was probably not for me.

On the other hand, I recognize that there can be some beautiful exceptions to this rule. For instance, Carrie Underwood is clearly one of the best things *ever* to happen to our country music world. She's also been the best singer and CMA cohost that any guy could ever ask for. Country music clearly lucked out when she came our way after winning *American Idol*. That's because it's become clear that Carrie is making music for the right reasons, and she just keeps getting better and better. She is living proof of the po-

> *Yeah, baby. That was my freestyle dance routine. I moonwalked.*

tential of some of these shows to enhance our lives in ways we don't expect. By virtue of her talent and hard work, she's gradually become an American idol the old-fashioned way too.

SOLO

I was lucky enough to go on tour with Brad a few years ago. Through that and through our adventures in co-hosting the CMA Awards, he has become like a big brother to me. You know, like that pesky big brother who does nothing but pick on you and pick on his guitar! At least one of those pays off real well. Of course, if I had a real big brother, I would want him to be just like Brad. And, let's face it, there's no better player I know.

—CARRIE UNDERWOOD

My friend Carrie has handled getting famous on camera on a weekly basis with amazing grace, just like everything else she does. On the other hand, I don't think I would have ever won *American Idol* or even made it through those auditions. Instead, I was granted the time and space to build my success story slow and steady over the course of years. Instead of facing judges on TV right away, I faced live audiences of all shapes and sizes from a very young age. In my experience, the people in those hometown crowds teach you much of what you ultimately need to know as a performer and an entertainer. And they don't hit a gong or a buzzer when you fail. Or vote you out of town.

To steal a phrase from a Miranda Lambert song, I was famous in a small town. Growing up as a local player in Glen Dale, I had plenty of time to get ready for the big time. For the record, Glen Dale does have a few interesting claims to fame—for example, Baseball Hall of Famer George Brett was born there, and I recently found out Lady Gaga's mother went to John Marshall High School. I'm sure they're repainting the WELCOME TO GLEN DALE sign as we speak.

WELCOME TO GLEN DALE

HOME OF LADY GAGA'S MOTHER

and Brad Paisley

I feel very fortunate that what little fame I could muster up in my small town came without my having to chase it too hard. As far as I can remember, I never had to beg to play anywhere. People just kept asking me, and I actually had to turn a lot of work down. On my path, every opportunity that came my way basically came from doing the work. Work begat work—which is an excellent way to learn your trade.

I had a healthy little look at show business. It also helped that I didn't have parents or anyone else in my circle looking at me like I was their big meal ticket or some way to live out some vicarious dream. After all, a C-Note only goes so far—even in a place like Glen Dale.

Work begat work— which is an excellent way to learn your trade.

Every single crowd at every single gig—good, bad, and ugly—taught me something, even when there really wasn't much of a crowd. *Especially* when there wasn't much of a crowd. Now, that doesn't mean that I wouldn't be a little pain and complain sometimes. My mother reminded me recently about a time when I was booked to play guitar at Oglebay Park in nearby Wheeling, West Virginia, around Christmas for the bus tours that would come by. I would have to leave school a little early for these gigs, and yet sometimes there would only be one or two people out there listening. That's just about the only time my mom remembers me asking why I was doing this anyway. My father rightly pointed out that I would have gladly traded that specific hundred-dollar bill for another hundred audience members. Thinking back on it now, those were important shows because even at an early age, they taught me the important lesson of living up to your deals.

Ironically—considering that I was technically a child myself at the time—one of the worst gigs that I remember doing was at the public library for a bunch of little kids during story hour. I recall leaving school one day a little early to play there for a bunch of preschoolers who were not much older than my kids are now. For the first time ever, I totally and obviously *bombed*. Nuclear.

I can remember desperately pulling out "Jingle Bells" (in the summertime), the theme from *Sesame Street,* the "Hokey Pokey," and anything else I thought might work with this tough crowd, but I could do absolutely nothing right that afternoon. To older audiences, my relative youth and old-school style might have been charming, but to these tykes I guess I just looked like some old hack. I was eleven or twelve at the time, and I remember my mom driving me home afterward and knowing I'd missed the mark. My mom got in the car and said, "Well, umm, that didn't go too well."

And she was right, but at least I learned how to keep playing through the pain—a necessary lesson as a guitarist and performer.

I am proudest of the times I spent playing for people in need, even at that early age. There was always a benefit somewhere, thrown by a guy like County Commissioner Biggie Byard, where they were raising money for a family or two, and they needed guitarists. Hank and I would always go back people up for those events or for nursing home performances or children's charities. I was always getting requests like that. And my parents saw to it that I never turned down these chances to help people. Mom and Dad made sure of that. It was their way of helping me keep some perspective in this crazy dream of mine. Once a month I would go play for the respite care floor of the local hospital. I remember a woman who was one of the residents there; she had suffered a stroke. I was only eleven or so, and seeing this sort of reality was life-changing. This woman could no longer speak a word, but she could sing along perfectly with "You Are My Sunshine" or "In the Garden." I would sit by her hospital bed and strum the chords on my guitar while she belted out the words clearly and effortlessly. Otherwise she would just stare. It was very heavy stuff. My visits to perform were some of the highlights of her life at that point. I knew that. And somehow I've never looked at music the same.

In general, I think that my parents were a little baffled by the actions of their guitar-crazy only son. They were always supportive, even if they had no clue about the music or entertainment businesses. Yet before long it became clear that my dad, in particular, really loved being with me on this musical journey. My dad has never been a stage parent, and he's not living any of his unaccomplished dreams through me. More than anything, I'd say that he just wanted to hop on the bus and come along for the ride. From the start, Dad drove me around and learned how to set up a PA system because somebody had to. And after I became a touring artist, he got his commercial driver's license and started to relief-drive the bus. Apparently, you *can* teach some old dogs new tricks.

Being a schoolteacher, my mom worried a little more about her son the musician. But from the sixth grade on, I had a plan. And studying anything other than the *Mel Bay Guitar Book* was not part of it. My grades started to suffer, and so did my mother. She used to beg me to try a little harder in school. But the point was pretty much moot by the time I was eleven or twelve. That's because just as I was on the brink of becoming a genuine American teenager and probably even more insufferable than I already was, I accidentally fell into the single greatest musical education that a young guitar player could ever have—live radio. And I got there by the power of the pen.

I was twelve when I wrote my first song. Somehow, out of nowhere, I had an overwhelming urge to do just that. I don't remember much about the experience, just playing it for my parents the night I finished it. I think they were shocked. Looking back at it, *I'm* even shocked. It's way better than it ought to be. I've written worse songs in the last few years. It was called "Born on Christmas Day," and I started to perform it that Christmas.

One day the music director of WWVA—a wonderful man named Tom Miller—came to a Rotary Club luncheon in town to do a little local weather report as a joke. The headmaster of my junior high school, who was also speaking at the lunch, asked me to represent the school and sing a song. It was around the holidays, and so I knew just what to sing.

After the luncheon, Tom came up to me and said, "You have to come on *Jamboree USA* this week and do that song." I was floored. The Wheeling Jamboree was the big time, the mack daddy of places you could perform in my area. I took the news with complete maturity—I ran through the house that night when I got home and screamed.

Here's another of those amazing strokes of good luck that came to me inexplicably. Right place, right time. Or more accurately, divine intervention. Thankfully, I happened to have grown up only twenty minutes away from the Wheeling Jamboree, which was the second-oldest continually running barn dance and country radio broadcast, right after the Grand Ole Opry show itself. The Wheeling Jamboree was broadcast weekly on a 50,000-watt transmitter from an awesome old Victorian venue called the Capitol Theatre and could be heard by country fans across the entire Northeast.

Playing the Jamboree was almost like being on the Grand Ole Opry, only I didn't have to leave home to do it. They even had one of those classic microphone stands that read:

J
A
M
B
O
R
E
E

U
S
A

down the front of it.

The vast majority of the biggest stars in country music all came through Wheeling as part of the national circuit, but because the Jamboree wasn't in Nashville, where so many of the great artists lived, the format was a little different. Members of the Jamboree from the area played for about an hour to get things going, then a popular national headlining act played one or two shows depending on who that headliner was. I remember that a true country legend like George Jones would play two or three shows to packed houses. The great Charley

Pride would do as many as four sellout shows in a weekend and he'd add a matinee too. There was such a fan base in West Virginia for classic country that people were always lined up around the block in those days.

I was already a fan of the Wheeling Jamboree before I could even dream of actually being part of the action on-stage. One time my grandfather won tickets, and he took me with him to see the country star John Conlee. John had lots of popular country hits, like "Common Man," "Backside of Thirty," and "Lady Lay Down." As the show was wrapping up, my grandfather whispered to me that we should leave and try to beat the traffic. I begged Papaw to stay just a little longer because I knew that John Conlee hadn't sung his best song yet—"Rose Colored Glasses." My grandfather halfheartedly agreed to wait, and afterward on the way home he told me that I had good taste in songs. I was already interested in what made a country song work, but now that I had confirmation that I had good taste, I was fascinated.

Returning to the Jamboree—which had helped make me a fan of so many country music artists—to take the stage myself while I was still a kid was just unbelievable. Turns out it also was pretty unbelievable for the man who ran the music on the show. Many years later, the musical director of the Wheeling Jamboree Zane Baxter confessed to me that he was completely furious when he heard that Tom Miller had invited a little boy from Glen Dale to come onto the radio program. He'd asked Tom that very night, "Is this going to be the worst thing that we have ever done?"

For whatever reason, Tom Miller went out on a limb for me and said, "Well, I don't think so, but I'm willing to go out there and introduce the kid, so don't worry. Let me take the responsibility for this. I'll take the blame if he's awful. But I really think you'll be surprised."

I was already interested in what made a country song work, but now that I had confirmation that I had good taste, I was fascinated.

Fortunately, I didn't know a thing about any of this backstage drama at that time.

I was the most excited I had ever been as I walked out on the stage of the Jamboree. Only my guitar was there to help take on the biggest audience I had ever faced. I caught my breath and started to play and sing my only hit—"Born on Christmas Day," a song I still love. Because I was very young, or not completely horrible, or possibly some combination of the two, the Jamboree audience gave a wonderful and welcoming reception. That very night, Zane Baxter changed his tune and invited me to return soon. Zane later told me that what really made him take notice of me that night was the fact that here was this young kid who dared to sing an original Christmas song rather than one of the obvious standards. And he could tell I could *play*. Really play. Especially for thirteen years old.

There's an important lesson there. If I had gone out there, strummed, and sung something safe, like, say, "Winter Wonderland," I can't imagine that the Jamboree would have been as impressed. Or ever ended up inviting me back on the show to be their new, young regular performer. It was the fact that I dared to write and play my own song that made the powers that be sit up and take notice and give me this big and crazy break. Ever since then, I think I've always seen the writing as the thing that has pushed me forward to the next level as an artist.

Being a part of the Jamboree as a teenager was a dream come true. Our job was to warm up the audience for our headliner. That's how, as a teenager, I got the unique career-altering chance to open for so many of the greats. By the time I was sixteen, I was playing the Jamboree every other weekend—or every weekend—and I played in the band some too, which was good for learning my chops as a player.

Those were *my* American Saturday nights for a good long time. I'll never forget those shows and all the greats who I got to open for. Though I can hardly believe it as I write a few of these names on a list, I got to open for George Jones, Conway Twitty, Charley Pride, Vince Gill, Steve Wariner, Charlie Daniels, Little Jimmy Dickens, Chet Atkins (twice), Larry Gatlin and the Gatlin Brothers, Ricky Skaggs, John Conlee (twice), Ray Stevens, Lee Greenwood, Joe Diffie, the Desert Rose Band, Exile, the Judds . . . I could go on and on.

So many of the headlining stars were kind and generous and complimentary to me. Especially Charley Pride. When Charley came to headline at the Jamboree, he was usually nice enough to slip into the audience and watch the first part of the show. It's hilarious to me to think that this African-American superstar could possibly not stand out in the all-white country crowd assembled to watch him play in Wheeling. One night my mom and her friend Susan were excited to notice that Charley Pride was sitting right there in front of them. When I came out onstage picking and singing, Charley Pride turned around and asked, "Excuse me, who is that?" My mom got shy, but Susan said, "That's her son." Afterward, Charley said, "Your son's amazing. I want to meet him."

That's how we all first met, and Charley exchanged numbers with us and struck up a phone friendship with my father. He wanted to help me if he could. To this day, Charley still has my dad's number. In fact, Charley might have been the very first big country artist who took a real interest in me— and the first to ever tell my father that I had something special and should come to Nashville and take my shot at becoming a recording artist.

Charley—one of twelve children of a poor sharecropper from Mississippi—became a groundbreaking country superstar, thanks to his famously smooth baritone on thirty-six number one hits, including "I'm Just Me," "Kiss an Angel Good Morning," and "My Eyes Can Only See as Far as You." This was a man who was tearing up the charts during the height of the racial tensions in our country. In fact, his record label at the time used to ship singles with no photo of Charley. I've heard that the first time he played the Opry, Charley walked out to a huge ovation, which abruptly stopped. He walked silently to the mic and, with total grace and humor, said, "Think of it as a permanent suntan." And the ice was forever broken. What a pioneer. Many years later, I was honored to play with Charley Pride at the White House for President Obama and the First Lady. That night, Charley went straight up to my father and said, "Doug, is your number still . . . ," and then told my dad his number correctly.

A lot of the famous headliners would hear about this teenager who was pretty good and would actually watch me play. I'll never forget being thirteen and seeing the Judds—who were really rocking my world and the rest of the world back then—standing on the side of the stage taking an interest in *my* act.

Country music was then—and still is—an overwhelmingly warm, welcoming community chock-full of some of the nicest folks you could ever want to meet. The headliners were always more than willing to be cordial to an aspiring young talent. I can't believe the things I got to see at that show. From the amplifiers and guitar gear the greats used, to Chet Atkins sitting around backstage pickin', to Vern Gosdin so furious with his monitors that he threw his cup of beer in the air, which completely soaked yours truly. Now, that's a baptism.

Thankfully, very few bottles came my way, and I still have some of the photos of me with all these country greats when I was just a kid. Some of my most treasured are photos of me at twelve with Vince Gill and Steve Wariner, who were just then becoming my heroes as singers, songwriters, and, more importantly, guitarists. Meeting these giants and sharing a stage with them was my first real hint that maybe this was not an impossible dream. I was at least in the vicinity. Perhaps I really could become a player.

As an American musician, I hold this truth to be self-evident: a guitar makes a better friend than most human beings. Seriously, some of my best friends are guitars. But right about this point in my coming-of-age as a man and a musician, I started to notice something beyond guitars . . . amplifiers.

Disclaimer: These next few paragraphs are probably going to be boring for anyone not interested in guitar gear. You've been warned.

That's right: I was a teenage amp-head. Suddenly it dawned on me that as much as I loved guitars, the amp was often 75 percent of the equation. My grandfather had started me off small with a little Fender amp that was just fine for a while, but then I convinced my father that I needed to have a Fender Twin—and I needed it on wheels, too, because it weighed about a hundred and fifty pounds, and my father, who had to carry it most of the time, only weighed a

As an American musician, I hold this truth to be self-evident: a guitar makes a better friend than most human beings.

hundred and fifty pounds himself. But just when my father thought I would be satisfied with that, I decided unilaterally that I needed—that's *needed,* mind you, not wanted—a Mesa Boogie pre-amp and amp with two speakers and a big rack full of junk with blinking lights to go with it. I was a kid in a candy store playing at that Jamboree. I would see these guys come through with their fancy rigs and flashy guitars, and my saliva glands would activate. I had Fender amps, then Peavey amps, then pedal boards, then rack gear, then wireless units— you name it.

All of this high fidelity and high finance pales in comparison to what my father and I call the Great Vox Amp Crisis of 1987. That's the year when I came to Dad at age fifteen to explain to him in no uncertain terms that I now needed—again, not wanted, but *needed*—some very specific and hard-to-find Vox amps from England. My father had begun to realize that something was going on a little earlier when he noticed that his phone bill was suddenly full of long and expensive phone calls to Great Britain because I had done due diligence and discovered the numbers of some excellent music stores across the Atlantic.

These amps were the stuff of legend, first made famous by the Shadows and the Beatles, and they were rare and mythical in late-eighties West Virginia. They looked as exotic as a Ferrari to me with their basket-weave tolex, diamond grill cloth, chicken-head tone knobs, and blue bulldog speakers. And like I was Veruca Salt in *Charlie and the Chocolate Factory*, they were my golden goose. I had to have them. "How much, Wonka? Won't take no for an answer. Come now, how much, I say? Now, now, everything is for sale . . ." And they were going to be mine.

My sudden and overwhelming interest in calling England first started when I opened up for my new favorite group, the Desert Rose Band, an incredibly innovative country band formed by Chris Hillman, formerly of the Byrds, and featuring the apex of my all-time guitar heroes, John Jorgenson, who would go on to play for years with Elton John and record or tour with everyone from Hank Williams Jr. to Luciano Pavarotti. As soon as I realized that the Desert Rose Band had Vox amps, I scammed someone into giving me John Jorgenson's phone number. So I just called John blind and said, "My name is Brad Paisley. I opened for you at the Jamboree in Wheeling, and I love your sound. Do you have a minute to talk about Vox amps?" Rather than just hang up on this punk, John was nice enough to explain that you could only get these amplifiers in certain places and that I wanted the old ones, not the new ones. He told me there was a great music store in Louisville that would probably have them, but that they'd have a lot more to choose from in England at certain stores.

Despite the fact that I would avoid math homework at all costs, I gladly calculated the time difference between Glen Dale, West Virginia, and Doncaster, England, even though I failed to properly calculate the cost per minute. The first time I heard a British phone go *burr-burr* instead of *ring, ring,* I freaked out. Then someone with an actual British accent answered and I really got giddy. I pulled myself together and explained that I was interested in getting some Vox AC30s, and by any chance did he have any? This unimpressed guy with a thick British accent said, "Yes. We've got about *fifty.*"

With my heart pounding a mile a minute, I somehow worked out a deal to buy two. I think the cost for my dream amplifiers came to $2,500 total. Not including the exorbitant phone bills. But hey, some kids my age were calling those late-night 900 numbers to hear heavy breathing by then, so I figure my parents should have been happy.

Dad also claims that I never paid him back for this sonic adventure, so I guess an eventual free Corvette is not accepted currency in these transactions. But by this point, I was earning $250 a pop playing solo for old ladies at a golf resort, so I did do a little of the math on that one.

After I made a deal in Doncaster, England, those Vox amps couldn't come in fast enough. In the end, it took them about two weeks to get to America, with me desperately tracking them all the way. I would lie awake at night and picture them crossing the Atlantic in the belly of a freighter, in their wooden shipping crates, like they were the lost ark and I was Indiana Jones about to intercept them. My new amps came through Pittsburgh to clear customs, and so my father and I decided to save a little money and drive there and get them ourselves in his Chevy Blazer. By now I was absolutely going out of my mind; I literally could not wait to get my hands on these amps. I had never really touched a Vox amp before—I had only seen them in concert and heard them on records— but I was already in love. No girl in school could be half as beautiful as these Vox amps were to me. Well, almost.

Finally we got to Pittsburgh and claimed my new musical treasure. I could not believe that I was now the proud owner of not one but two AC30s. By this point, customs had already torn the boxes apart looking for drugs or other contraband— unaware, perhaps, that these amplifiers *were* my drugs. Then

I furiously continued their work and ripped open the box to see the head control plate and know for sure that I had actually gotten what I (or rather, my dad) had paid for—and blissfully discovered that I had.

Dad and I loaded the amp boxes into his car, and we drove all the way home through the snow in the frigid air. Then right as we arrived in Glen Dale, my father—who's a volunteer fireman in our little town—decided we had to stop by the firehouse and wash the salt from the highway off the Chevy. By this point, I was just dying because I was literally one half mile away from my house—and from my dream of playing my first Vox AC30s. And they were right there in the boot. (That's British for "trunk." Pip pip. Read on.) It was around seven thirty P.M. and getting very dark. In just an hour or so, it would be too late to play for fear of waking up the neighbors. Anyway, I was losing my mind. My father, on the other hand, was enjoying every minute of seeing me in agony as he carefully cleaned his vehicle. Payback can take many forms other than money.

At long last, we got back to our house around nine. I was flipping out because this was my ultimate dream coming true. It was like a Christmas morning moment for me. I tore apart those boxes and rushed to plug a guitar into one of my new

Voxes because I had never even heard one up close. And then came a moment of pure horror—despite all my research and calculations and conversions, it was not until that exact second that I made a horrible realization: British amps came with . . . British electrical plugs!

Try as I might, I couldn't plug either of my new amps in. So we ran down to the hardware store to try to get some kind of adapter. By the time we got back and got the right AC cords attached, it was so late that I could barely turn the amps up because of old Mr. and Mrs. Cerra next door, but at least I was touching my amp and it was powered up and I could sneak off a few notes. I played three chords, they rang out like the sounds I imagine Saint Peter will greet us all with when we reach the pearly gates, and it was just too much. I blew a fuse. No, seriously, I blew a fuse in the amp. As it turned out, the next trip to the hardware store would be for fuses. We got to know the chap at True Value well over the next few days. Anyway, I had discovered my sound. My tone. It had arrived here by boat, from the United Kingdom, much like my own ancestors centuries before.

As I prepared to graduate from John Marshall High School and think about my future, there could be no doubt that, musically speaking, my fuse was now already lit.

Guitar Tips from Brad

LESSON #4

Don't play mad—but if you do, play *furious*.

5

THE CLIFFS
OF ROCK CITY

Everything I ever really needed to know about playing guitar I learned before I graduated from high school. All those days and nights when I was so busy not doing my homework and not going on hot dates, I was actually doing something very important. In retrospect, I was growing the deep musical roots that have put me where I am today—wherever that might be.

Back in junior high, most other kids weren't all that impressed by this little odd kid with big ears and an even bigger guitar who had somehow developed the bizarre ability to "chicken pick." It was pretty hard to excite my peer group by playing a jazz standard like "Cherokee" or maybe some bluegrass classic like "Salty Dog" that they didn't know.

My musical repertoire back then was decidedly too old-fashioned for their young ears and more likely to thrill my teachers, my parents, and even my grandparents than it was to charm my classmates. I was a young man out of time and out of fashion. So as high school rolled around, I began to expand my horizons. I had to come up with some way to impress my classmates, especially the female ones. And it wasn't going to be with "Wildwood Flower."

So like all kids will do, I started to discover popular music. But I could tell right away what I liked and didn't like. I was instantly attracted to any song with a great guitar part. That would remain true to this day. Conversely, if there wasn't much by way of "pickin' " in a pop song, my attention went out the door. Luckily, this was the late eighties. There was a plethora of pickin'. *Every* rock band had its virtuoso lead player. Van Halen had Eddie, Bon Jovi had Richie, AC/DC had Angus, ZZ Top had Billy, Toto had Luke, Spinal Tap had Nigel, and Eric Clapton had it all. I devoured this stuff. I found that with the background I'd been given learning jazz runs alongside Hank every night and a distortion pedal patched in front of the amp, I was not far off. I might have even been slightly ahead of the curve. When my friends would come over, they would beg me to break into "Layla" or "Eruption" or "La Grange." I could play something as complicated as Jerry Reed's "The Claw," and they would sit there unimpressed. But something as brainless and simple as the riff from "Smoke on the Water," and they would absolutely lose their minds. I loved the feeling of playing something on the guitar that would make my friends flip out. The only problem was that when I would sing, it didn't much sound like Kiss or Van Halen or Eric Clapton or even Spinal Tap. Well, maybe Spinal Tap. So here I was, a burgeoning rock guitarist trapped in a country singer's body. What to do?

When I was growing up, our little part of West Virginia felt like a kind of musical crossroads. There was lots of country music on the radio—everything from the Judds to Dwight Yoakam—and there was a whole lot of classic rock. Of course, back then it was just rock. The "classic" hadn't officially been added to the name yet. I loved rock music. But I also loved country. Real country. Being a fan of country music made me happy, but it also made me a slightly odd young man. Frankly, most of the other kids at my high school seemed a lot more interested in listening to me play Van Halen licks in my living room than they did in hearing me play on the same stage as Vern Gosdin at the Wheeling Jamboree.

> *I loved the feeling of playing something on the guitar that would make my friends flip out.*

I get it. Eddie Van Halen blew me away, too, and he still does. What I especially loved about Eddie Van Halen's high-flying style was that the guitar was so absolutely central to his band's sound. When you listened to Van Halen, you could tell the guitar player was at least as important as the lead singer in this group—maybe more so. Heck, Van Halen would go on to replace their lead singer a few times, but they could *never* replace Eddie Van Halen. I loved the idea of a guitarist being at the center of any band.

Back in the late eighties, the relatively wholesome nature of country music had a bit of a hard time competing with the more dangerous-sounding thrills of "Running with the Devil" in rock and roll. There were times when I felt like a country kid living in an MTV world. But in 1989, when I started high school, little did I know that our little musical world was about to change in a very big way. A seismic shift was about to take place in the musical landscape, and that change went by the name of Garth Brooks.

Along with Clint Black and a few other popular country artists, Garth Brooks came along and set the woods on fire with country music. Not just the woods actually, but the whole damn city too. Garth did a lot to make country instantly cool for a whole new generation of fans, including a lot of young people who had never liked it before. Suddenly, wearing a cowboy hat was all the rage—even in towns where they didn't have any actual cows.

Thanks to my grandfather, I was already a devoted disciple of country music by this point. I didn't have to jump on any country music bandwagon because I was already firmly on board. Country music always has been—and always would be—cool with me. But Garth Brooks came along and broke down barriers. He became a kind of red-hot musical supernova seen by millions of new country music fans everywhere.

For a country star, he really rocked.

Beyond all that, Garth Brooks did something truly remarkable—specifically for me. Against all odds, Garth Brooks somehow managed to single-handedly make Brad Paisley much more popular in high school.

Here's how he did it: When Garth became the biggest star in music, all of a sudden the cooler kids at school who knew I played guitar started coming up to me and saying, "Hey, Paisley, can *you* play any of that Garth Brooks stuff?" Not being a complete idiot—despite what my report card at the time might have suggested—I quickly told them all, "Sure, I can."

Of course, I already knew those songs. After all, like the

rest of the world, I was a Garth fan too. Before long, some of the songs on country radio were just as cool to these kids as "You Shook Me All Night Long" or "Hot for Teacher."

In a flash, I became a man in demand at John Marshall High School. Lots of guys and even some actual living, breathing high school girls started taking a newfound interest in my weekend plans. They'd come up to me at school and say things like, "Brad, so why don't you bring your guitar to our party?" Or, "So, do you ever do anything besides sing and play on the weekends?" All of a sudden, I found myself with a social life. It was like something out of a Michael Cera movie.

Overnight, I went from being that nerdy Paisley kid playing with those old farts at the street fair to that cool Paisley guy with the guitar who could sing and play "Friends in Low Places" around the campfire.

You know, over the years Garth has gone out of his way to say some very nice things about yours truly, and I would like to take this opportunity to thank him for everything he's done for me. Without you, Garth Brooks, it's quite possible that I *still* would be wondering what it's like to kiss an actual girl. I thank you, and my children thank you.

Garth brought a rock and roll energy to the country music world, but at heart, the songs Garth sang in stadiums had us all singing along because he understood instinctively what makes country music work on any scale. As he once put it, "True country music is honesty, sincerity, and real life to the hilt." In the late eighties and nineties, Garth took real life to the hilt, and in the process, he made my real life a whole lot better too.

Here's yet another time in my life when I experienced perfect timing and what can only be described as a certain amount of pure dumb luck. Almost exactly at the precise moment when I was starting to discover the opposite sex, the opposite sex was discovering country music. Just by being a cowboy who owned a guitar, I somehow became popular by association.

It was obvious right away, even to me, that the simple act of holding a guitar made me a whole lot more interesting, even attractive, to girls. No, I still didn't have quite enough confidence or game, but now I could at least see my best hope for avoiding complete loneliness. After all, at that age, everybody is just trying to find some angle on life. I think everyone in high school feels like a nerdy, awkward teenager, but at least I was a nerdy, awkward teenager with one very effective, shiny crutch—the kind that came with six nickel strings attached.

Sometimes I'll run into country music fans, and they ask me, "You know what I like about you?" I usually respond with "Hopefully more than just one thing, but go on."

"I like that you can really play the guitar."

Taking a cue from the Van Halen playbook, the guitar is the center of my band. It's really the center of my music in general. It is such a huge part of the thought process behind my records. To this day, when I take a solo in a song, I like to include something that's unique. Sometimes it may not sound too hard, but I always love it when I meet a guitar player and he or she says something like, "I have *never* been able to figure out how you do that part in 'Water' " or ". . . in 'Ticks.' " I love those conversations, and I love being able to discuss tricks of the trade with kindred souls. I also enjoy the look that comes over their faces when that lightbulb goes off and they look like they can't wait to get home and play that lick for themselves after having talked. It's an empowering moment. There is nothing like the feeling that your music has been an inspiration for another musician.

I spend some of my time in Santa Barbara, California, these days, and I'll never forget the first time I went into the store Instrumental Music there. I walked in, and a teenager and his dad started staring. Here was a kid looking a lot like I used to look: rock and roll T-shirt, 108 pounds, clean-cut, Dad in tow. It really was some sort of déjà vu seeing this kid with his old-man chauffeur just starting out. I walked over and said, "Hi." The dad laughed and said, "Well, you're not going to believe this, but he's here for his guitar lesson, and he's learning 'Old Alabama' today. He learned 'This Is Country Music' last week. We've seen you in concert five times. What in the world are you doing here?" I told them that I live there part of the time. Oh, and that "Old Alabama" is in the key of G. The son then asked if I would meet his instructor, so I said sure.

I had a great little conversation about my playing with the instructor, who was responsible for deciphering the ridiculous things I come up with in the studio for his student. I know what it's like to try to learn my licks; I have to do it every time I finish an album. That teacher had a lot of respect for me, but I wasn't sure if he wanted to hug me or hit me.

The guitar is the center of my band. It's really the center of my music in general.

I love being a popular guitar player.

By the same token, I also love it when I put a guitar part in a song that gets popular. Then I know that any band that tries to play that song at Robert's Western World on Broadway in Nashville cannot leave it out of their rendition. Like in "Old Alabama"; I dare anyone to try to play that song without my, Randy Owen's, and Jeff Cook's guitar parts. To me those guitar parts are part of the DNA of the song, a living breathing thing. Somewhere tonight, someone else is playing them. And those notes will forever have a life of their own.

I think my focus on the importance of the guitar parts in my records and in my band comes from Buck Owens.

In my grandfather's home, Buck Owens was definitely not simply that loveable character on *Hee Haw* but a towering figure in American music. In fact, come to think about it, Roy Clark, another world-class player in country and a great classical guitarist to boot, also hosted *Hee Haw*, and I partly learned guitar by studying one of Roy's books that taught his guitar method.

Say what you will about *Hee Haw*, but there sure was a whole lot of guitar talent in Kornfield Kounty. In our house, we watched *Hee Haw* every week, and I think it was such a fantastic showcase for music. There may have been some downside for both Buck and Roy—*Hee Haw* painted both of them as jocular TV hosts as opposed to serious musicians, which they most assuredly were by any standard. On any given week, we all got to see their obvious musical genius, but of course, we also got to see them dressed in overalls, with a piece of straw in their mouths, looking like complete hillbillies—which I personally *loved*. In retrospect, I can understand that it may not have been the best idea for these musicians in terms of creating mystique. But in the end, I know this: *Hee Haw* made millions of people across the country happy—including everyone in my family—and it exposed people in towns large and small to *tons* of great music. It taught me something wonderful about how fantastic the combination of country music and comedy could be.

More than just about anything else, falling in love with the music of Buck Owens and the Buckaroos widened my understanding of music by introducing me to the very aggressive, really twangy Telecaster sound that Buck championed along with Don Rich, the resident guitar god in his groundbreaking band. Listening to Buck Owens and the Buckaroos was my unforgettable introduction to the whole Bakersfield sound that also included another one of my heroes, Merle Haggard, and his band the Strangers, featuring the great Roy

Nichols on guitar. I gravitated toward that honky-tonk Tele-caster sound immediately. Little did I know then that some-day I would be able to call Buck Owens a friend and mentor, and that I would get to stand with Vince Gill and honor Merle Haggard in front of an American president at the Kennedy Center Honors.

Beyond being one of my greatest musical heroes, Buck Owens was a truly incredible friend, and, for me, was a larger-than-life presence. One of my earliest musical memo-ries is listening to "Tiger by the Tail" on the turntable with my grandfather and running around in circles whenever that song would play. Something about Buck's records drove me crazy in the best possible way. Buck's sound was always so infectious and his two-part harmony that he did with Don Rich was stunning and powerful. The music of Buck Owens and the Buckaroos was everything that I love: here was great, vivid, lived-in country music without any saccharine, with-out being watered down. This music was unashamed coun-try with a lot of attitude—honky-tonk twang and proud of it. His music even sounded like a bar somehow. It sounded like beer. It sounded like cigarette smoke. It sounded like grown-ups having a really good time in ways that I could barely even imagine—though I confess I tried my best. Buck Owens and the Buckaroos' music sounded like heaven to my ears, and maybe a little bit of hell too.

Either way, I wanted in badly. Come to think of it, I still do.

Buck Owens was such a hero to me that many years later when I finished my first album, *Who Needs Pictures,* in 1999, I asked my record label, Arista Nashville, to send an early copy to Buck with a note attached from me explaining that he was a tremendous influence on me and that I hoped he'd be able to hear that in my music.

I was just content that my hero would hear my album and hopefully notice somehow what he meant to me.

Before long, Buck got in touch with me through Jerry Hufford, who worked for him and ran his famous club in Bakersfield, the Crystal Palace. Buck had heard my album, called Jerry, and said, "Did this guy *really* play all these guitars?"

So Jerry called me up and told me, "Buck wants to know if you really played all those guitar parts."

I proudly said, "Yes."

And Jerry said, "Buck says, '*Bullshit.*' "

I've never been more thrilled to hear that word. I assured Jerry that yes, I really did play all that stuff.

Soon after that, Jerry called back and said, "Buck says, 'Prove it,' " and wanted to know if I would come out to the Crystal Palace and sit in with the Buckaroos. Without missing a beat, I answered, "Say when." Then I got on the next plane to Bakersfield to spend the weekend. I had never even been to Bakersfield before, and this was definitely the right way to go there—being personally summoned to the Palace by the king himself.

Once I got there, I was immediately invited to sit in with Buck and play guitar at the Crystal Palace. I think Buck was floored to see for himself what a deep influence he and Don Rich had been on me. I have a picture of Buck pointing at me onstage saying, "Take it, kid," much the same way Hank Goddard used to do. Our friendship started that day, and it became one of the most thrilling and meaningful of my entire career.

I have a picture of Buck pointing at me onstage saying, "Take it, kid," much the same way Hank Goddard used to do.

Buck Owens turned out to be everything I dreamed he would be and more. Eccentric, loud, charming, larger than life, funny, and above all, generous.

After that, whenever I found myself in California, I always tried to go up to Bakersfield and either sit in with the band or just have lunch with Buck. I remember days off between fairs and festivals on the early touring circuit when I would rush up there just to grab dinner, pick his brain, and hear his fantastic stories about playing with Don Rich and the guys.

One year on December 27 or so, Nashville was in the middle of an incredible ice storm. A psycho girlfriend had just broken up with me, and so I desperately wanted to spend New Year's Eve somewhere else, anywhere else. Preferably somewhere warm. I called up Jerry Hufford at the Crystal Palace and said, "What's Buck doing for New Year's?"

"Just playing here," he said.

"Ask him if he wants me to be his Don Rich for the evening."

Next thing I knew, I was on a plane for Bakersfield to sit in. I got to live out the fantasy of being the right-hand man in the best band ever assembled in country music, and I got to get that girl off my mind. Just like Papaw had predicted, that guitar of mine was getting me over things and into things.

Over the years, Buck and I got to record some stuff together and we also had lots of time to just hang out. I played New Year's Eve with him four different times. Here was a musical giant that the Beatles themselves covered, and he was willing to spend time with me. I treasured every second. Even though Buck was already a living legend by the time I got to know him, he still loved to talk guitar and music in general any time you wanted.

Some people forget that Buck Owens was a guitar player first. Buck was actually a respected L.A. guitarist back in the fifties, and he played on sessions for everyone from Faron Young to Wanda Jackson. Then Buck ran across a sixteen-year-old Don Rich playing fiddle in a bar in Tacoma, Washington. Buck quickly realized that Don was better than he was as a guitar player, so Buck decided that his role was to be the band's front man, strum rhythm guitar, and play the occasional lead part.

Buck had the vision and the humility to basically turn the guitar spotlight over to this other amazing musician with his own signature sound.

Don Rich was part of a very rare breed. A pioneer of the Fender Telecaster, along with James Burton, also a guitar legend who famously played with Ricky Nelson, Elvis Presley, and later John Denver—just to name just a few.

Back when he was a kid, James Burton grabbed a Telecaster and decided to do some really unique string-bending with it that was unlike anything anyone had ever done before. He broke one pattern and started another. So much of that cool guitar sound that you might associate with rockabilly and country music really started with James Burton.

Don Rich piled on top of James Burton's revolutionary sound brilliantly and added his own thing too. Don understood the sort of twangy sound that suited Buck's voice and his style of song perfectly. What Don played with Buck was so powerful and innovative that along with James, Don blazed a trail for all of the twangy Telecaster players who have followed—of which I'm proud to be one.

Take a listen to the *Carnegie Hall Concert* album by Buck Owens and His Buckaroos from 1966—my favorite album of all time. Don is so fiery and so creative on this album and on everything he did that it still sounds fresh almost a half century later. Don was able to play anything from real country fiddle to great jazz guitar, and this gave him a real sense of adventurousness as a player. He took the guitar to some amazing and very entertaining places.

But Don died too soon in 1974 in a motorcycle accident on his way from a recording session in Bakersfield to a family vacation. Buck told me many times that beyond being this amazing musician, Don was also the nicest man you could imagine. Buck spoke to me often about the impact of that loss—not only of his greatest musical partner in crime but also his best friend. I think he was never quite the same after Don's death. I'm sure there was a feeling of closure on the era of music that they had so brilliantly created together. One of the true great duos in the history of music. I'll be thankful until the day I die that I got to know Buck Owens so well in his lifetime, but I wish that I could have met Don Rich too. You can tell watching the old videos what kind of presence Don had—beyond being a monster guitar player, he was a sweet man with an easy smile.

One of my guitar teachers, Roger Hoard in Wheeling, West Virginia—who was the lead guitar player on the Jamboree—did get to meet Don once. Roger told me about going to see Buck Owens and the Buckaroos when they came to West Virginia and played the Capitol Theatre. Roger was just a kid then, but he was already playing guitar. So Don Rich saw this boy waiting in the wings watching him and invited Roger to spend the day with him. He generously offered to listen to him play and gave him a few tips.

Time and time again, I've noticed that the greats of country music don't just have great skills but also great hearts.

When I joined the Opry at the Ryman back in 2001, I asked if I could wear Buck's yellow Carnegie Hall jacket. Buck

(left) A PORTRAIT OF THE ARTIST AS A YOUNG MAN WITH BIG EARS: Yes, that's really me—some time between my first and second birthday—on the front porch of our home in Glen Dale, West Virginia. *(Doug Paisley collection)*

(right) CATCH OF THE DAY: Years before "The Fishin' Song," I was already happily doing hours of serious research down at Sperling's Dock on the Ohio River in Glen Dale. *(Doug Paisley collection)*

THE BEGINNING: When I was eight years old, my late great Papaw—otherwise known as Warren is—gave me this Sears Danelectro guitar and changed my life forever. I can never thank him enough, 'm going to try. *(Doug Paisley collection)*

A ROOM OF ONE'S OWN: My parents generously allowed this young amp-head to have his own music room in our house in Glen Dale. Here I'm all set up for one of my first big recording ions. *(Doug Paisley collection)*

TEENAGE DREAM: Despite that baby face, I'm thirteen here and no doubt playing some tly hot licks in front of the Paisley home fireplace. *(Doug Paisley collection)*

(above, left) THE GREATEST GUITAR PLAYER YOU MAY NEVER HAVE HEARD OF: Here's my teacher, bandmate, and mentor, Clarence "Hank" Goddard. His musical genius and generosity of spirit set me on my way. As a man and a musician, Hank taught me so much of what I know today. *(Doug Paisley collection)*

(above, right) SHOWING OFF: My first brushes with the big time came playing as part of Jamboree USA at the Capitol Music Hall in Wheeling, West Virginia. Here, I'm fourteen years old. I'm not sure how good my playing was then, but my hair was fabulous. *(Doug Paisley collection)*

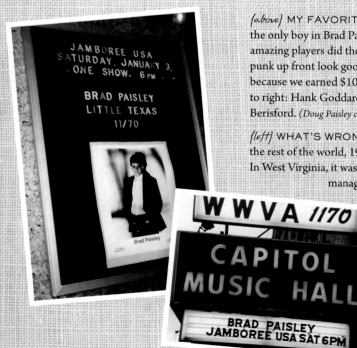

(above) MY FAVORITE BOY BAND: Okay, I was the only boy in Brad Paisley & the C-Notes, but the amazing players did their grown-up best to make the punk up front look good. We were called the C-Notes because we earned $100 for our first big gig. From left to right: Hank Goddard, Gene Elliott, and Tommy Berisford. *(Doug Paisley collection)*

(left) WHAT'S WRONG WITH THIS PICTURE: the rest of the world, 1991 was the year that grunge In West Virginia, it was my senior year when I some managed to get Little Texas to ope for me. Gentleme call your agents. (Paisley collection)

WHEN YOU'RE A CELEBRITY: knew that my nam had any marquee va whatsoever in 1990 Paisley collection)

ROLE MODEL AND FRIEND, THEN AND NOW: I first met Steve Wariner when he came to [...] in Wheeling in the eighties. He inspired me as a singer-songwriter and as a player. Here we are again [duri]ng the recording of the *Play* album honoring our musical mentors Chet Atkins and Hank Goddard. *([Dou]g Paisley and Brad Paisley collections)*

(below, counterclockwise)

ACT NATURAL: I may look calm enough here, but I'm overwhelmed to be playing with the one and only Buck Owens at the Crystal Palace in Bakersfield, California, on New Year's Eve right around the turn of the twenty-first century. Buck was a musical giant. I still cannot believe that I was able to call him my friend. *(Brad Paisley collection)*

SURROUNDED BY GREATNESS: Here I am with Hank Goddard and the legendary Chet Atkins. My grandfather would have loved this photo—even with that strange, stunned expression on my face. *(Doug Paisley collection)*

LITTLE BIG MAN: Right from the start, I've always been proud to stand beside my hero Little Jimmy Dickens, a giant talent with a huge heart and a fellow West Virginian. This photo was taken on a night when I opened for Jimmy in a high school gym in Harrisburg, Pennsylvania. *(Doug Paisley collection)*

YESTERDAY WHEN I WAS YOUNG AND TODAY WHEN I'M NOT: Here I am grinning with Roy Clark way back in the Jamboree days. Then in 2010, Roy generously joined us onstage to play "Ghost Riders in the Sky" in Tulsa, Oklahoma, during the last show of the year of our H20 World Tour. *(Doug Paisley collection) (Ben Enos)*

(left) SMILE AND SAY CHEESE: This is my first-ever PR photo. I'm not sure if I'm fourteen or fifteen here, but either way, I was definitely not cool. *(Doug Paisley collection)*

(right) GRADUATION DAY: Here I am with my wonderful parents, Doug and Sandy Paisley, the day that I got my diploma from Belmont University. Apparently none of us can quite believe that I made it this far—or possibly we're all remembering that unfortunate D I got in guitar my first semester. *(Doug Paisley collection)*

MISTER ROGERS: In the studio with my longtime producer and pal Frank Rogers. Usually we're working somewhat harder than this. *(Photograph © Tony Phipps)*

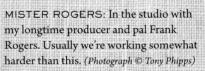

SUCCESS OR SOMETHING LIKE IT: At the platinum party for my *Who Needs Pictures* album with (from left) my then manager and still friend Jimmy Gilmer, Arista's Mike Dungan, and Frank Rogers. *(Photograph © Tony Phipps)*

URBAN RENEWAL: Playing around with the very talented Keith Urban in the early days and also on the set of our "Start a Band" video. How on earth are we superstars now? *(Brad Paisley collection) (Ben Enos)*

TIME WARP: Here are some of the key players in my life at a 2008 party celebrating 10 years in the business, 10 million albums sold, and 10 #1 singles. From left to right, some fine folks who helped make it all possible: Frank Rogers, Kelley Lovelace, ASCAP's Connie Bradley, some guy with a cowboy hat, Joe Galante, my dad, Doug Paisley, and Chris DuBois. *(Courtesy of Sony Music Nashville)*

PLAYING AROUND: Preparing to record for *Play* with Redd Volkaert, who played my wedding reception, among other very important gigs. To clarify, I'm the one on the left without the blue cap. *(Brad Paisley collection)*

IN THE PRESENCE OF A MASTER: Here I am with the Master of the Telecaster himself, James Burton. I was so honored that this groundbreaking player was part of our little "Cluster Pluck." *(Brad Paisley collection)*

(clockwise)

HONORING BUCK: Shortly after Buck Owens's death in 2006, I was proud to be asked to be part of a big tribute to my hero and friend at the Academy of Country Music Awards in Las Vegas. That's me with Billy Gibbons of ZZ Top and Dwight Yoakam. *(41st Annual Academy of Country Music Awards—Getty Images/Courtesy of the Academy of Country Music)*

ME AND MR. TELECASTER: Albert Lee was once named Best Country Guitarist by *Guitar Player* magazine, even though he comes from another country—namely England. Albert is one of my all-time guitar gods, and it was such a thrill to "Cluster Pluck" with him too. *(Brad Paisley collection)*

JUST TRYING TO KEEP UP: Playing with the astounding Robben Ford in Nashville in 2010. I was honored and slightly scared when Robben—who wrote "Oh Yeah, You're Gone" on *American Saturday Night* with me—came up to play with us during our show at the Bridgestone Arena. *(Ben Enos)*

A ROYAL AUDIENCE: Letting the good times roll with the amazing B. B. King while recording together for the *Play* album. His stories are almost as much fun as watching him play. *(Scott Scovill)*

I'M WITH THE BAND: The Desert Rose Band, that is. What a thrill to sit in with one of my favorite groups featuring one of my guitar heroes, John Jorgenson. And yes, I got to share a stage with the timeless Emmylou Harris too. *(Brian Tipton/CMT.com)*

(counterclockwise)

A GOOD GIG IN A NICE HOUSE:
On July 21, 2009, I was very honored to
participate in the Country Music Celebration
as part of the White House Music Series
hosted by First Lady Michelle Obama. I play
many nice venues, but the White House will
always be special. *(Ben Enos)*

BIG TIME: In August 2010, I played my
first stadium show as a headliner at Gillette
Stadium in Boston, Massachusetts. This
was the 7th Annual New England Country
Festival, which also featured performances
by Easton Corbin, Sara Evans, Darius Rucker,
and Jason Aldean and drew a sold-out crowd
of over 51,000 country fans. It was one of
those moments that was just beyond my
dreams. *(Ben Enos)*

NOT A PRETTY PICTURE: I took
this photograph of my fantastic band and
amazing crew at our first show after the flood
in 2010—a remarkable group effort that
made me proud. Perhaps their exhaustion
explains some of their questionable fashion
choices. *(Brad Paisley collection)*

A GRAND TIME: Jamming for joy with some of my all-time
heroes Ricky Skaggs, Vince Gill, and Steve Wariner to raise funds
for flood relief and to help celebrate the Opry's 85th anniversary.
(2010 © Grand Ole Opry, photograph by Joel Dennis)

THE CIRCLE IS UNBROKEN: After the flood, the legendary
Little Jimmy Dickens and I had the honor of returning the restored
six-foot circle of oak to the Opry stage. I'm playing my prewar
Martin acoustic that has a remarkable history of its own. *(2010 ©
Grand Ole Opry, photograph by Chris Hollo)*

THREE WISE GENTLEMEN: Backstage at the CMA Awards with my manager, Bill Simmons, and my booking agent, Rob Beckham. *(Ben Enos)*

MY FIRST PRODUCERS: Here I am with my parents, who have always been supportive and are now the best free babysitters I could ever imagine. *(Doug Paisley collection)*

SHE'S EVERYTHING: That's me with my beautiful wife, Kim, at the 2009 CMA Awards. I think she'll keep me. *(Curtis Hilbun)*

(above) CHILD'S PLAY: I love to see Huck and Jasper play, and sometimes the feeling is mutual. *(Brad Paisley collection)*

(left) A NIGHT TO REMEMBER: Being named Entertainer of the Year at the 2010 Country Music Association Awards was the perfect ending to one of t most memorable and meaningful evenings during my life in music. *(John Russell/CMA)*

sent Jerry Hufford with it on a plane to personally deliver it to me. There were many times when Buck would call me just to talk, and I could scarcely believe it. We'd talk about guitars, amps—and for me talking about amps with Buck Owens was about as much fun as I could ever have. I introduced him to my producer Frank Rogers, and Buck would call him too just to talk. We could not believe our good fortune. To the very end, Buck had an incredible passion for being a musician and for entertaining people.

I will never forget the business advice he gave me over the years. He was so conscious of saving money and being frugal that I know he worried about me managing my income. He'd seen so many of his contemporaries snort their fortunes up their noses or go broke on bad business deals. He had no tolerance for frivolous spending or decadence when it came to running a business. When we moved from being crammed on one bus to having several, we used to hide them from view whenever we played Bakersfield. We would park mine by the Crystal Palace and the others on the far side of a hotel out of view. He'd walk in and say, "I see you still have one bus. Thatta boy!" And he was always absolutely against chartering private jets.

On March 25, 2006, Buck played a Friday show at the

Crystal Palace with the Buckaroos, had his favorite meal of chicken fried steak, and drove home. He then passed away in his sleep. I think that's absolutely the way he would have wanted it.

And in his honor, I cashed a free ticket voucher I'd gotten from Southwest Airlines and flew for free to sing at his funeral.

I was also fortunate enough to be a young guitar player during a time when there was a whole new bumper crop of great singing, guitar-slinging players like Steve Wariner and Vince Gill.

I first met Steve Wariner when I was about eleven years old. Brent Long—a good friend of my dad's at the time who would later become my road manager—met Steve when he was traveling through our area. Brent worked at a sporting goods store and Steve is a huge basketball fan, so when Steve was in town, Brent would set Steve up with a basketball court to play on.

One day while I was trying on a pair of Saucony George Brett turf shoes, Brent said to me, "Do you know who Steve

Wariner is?" I told him I did. Brent told me, "Well, you've got to come see Steve's show at the Capitol this weekend. He and I have become good friends and I've told him about you."

This was around 1984. I wasn't all that familiar with Steve, because after all, he was a popular modern artist, and at eleven, I, of course, was a product of complete senior-citizen influence. If it wasn't considered classic country gold, I probably hadn't had it force-fed to me. So when I went to the show, right from the start I stood there with my jaw on the floor. Here was this guy with a red Strat singing *and* playing great songs, talking to the crowd and entertaining them, all while playing the bulk of the lead guitar

> *I didn't just set out to become a big Steve Wariner fan. I set out to become Steve Wariner.*

parts. This was the lightbulb moment for me—the exact second when I finally put it all together and understood that you really could do all that, and even do it all well. It was like I had been handed a mission.

I didn't just set out to become a big Steve Wariner fan. I set out to become Steve Wariner.

A year or two later, I somehow convinced my family to let me make a pilgrimage to the promised land, Nashville, Tennessee, with Brent, and we went to see Steve Wariner play at Twitty City, the theme park the great Conway Twitty had next to his home. Brent put together the whole trip. The car broke down on our way back through Kentucky, and then we got stuck in Mammoth Cave. I obviously learned nothing from this, because in the year 2000 Brent became my road manager and still is today. Anyway, the concert I went to see is one I'll never forget—not just because Steve was great, but because of his opening act that day, a new guy named Vince Gill.

SOLO

It has always been an honor for me to have Brad list me as an influence on him as a young guitar player. I remember when I was a kid and the people I admired. If and when I got to meet them—and if they were nice to me—I have never forgotten it to this day. My greatest wish is that the first time I met Brad I was nice to him. PS: Now the whole world knows what a great guitar player Brad is!

—VINCE GILL

Right from the first time I heard Vince sing "Turn Me Loose," I have been a fan. To me and countless other fans around the world, Vince can do no wrong, whether he's singing, playing, or talking. While I loved country guitar, I didn't know what I was going to do with it or who I was going to be. But Steve and Vince showed me the way and changed my life. They showed me you could be a lead guitarist and still be an entertainer. They were both unique and extraordinary talents, and they still are. Around the same time Ricky Skaggs, who had started to take over the electric guitar leads in his band, was on the radio as well. I had been given a clear-cut blueprint.

In terms of their guitar playing, as I said before, Steve comes from the Chet Atkins school. Steve was a bass player and bandleader for Chet for a little while and sort of got adopted by Chet. Vince was also close to Chet, so in a sense, these were the guys anointed to carry on a great tradition.

Both incorporate the finesse of the fingerpickers like Chet Atkins, add a little Les Paul–type jazz, and pepper it with hints of Albert Lee. The funny thing about a guy like Albert Lee is that he's this Brit who shows up with the coolest twangy chicken-pickin' technique anyone had ever seen.

Of all the places to breed a blistering country honky-tonk hillbilly picker, the UK ought to be way down the list. But he has a well-earned reputation as a true guitar player's guitar player. Albert is part of a great musical continuum: first, there was James Burton, Don Rich, and Roy Nichols; then in the seventies, along comes Albert Lee playing with a great artist like Emmylou Harris, and he's playing faster than you have ever heard anybody play at this point. Listen to a song like "Luxury Liner" or his version of "Country Boy," as I have a million times, and you'll be in awe of Albert Lee just like I am. Another gem of a bloke, Albert is a great example of a humble virtuoso—a master—known for his finger precision and hybrid picking style. If there is a common thread running between all of these players that I am talking about, it's humility. Guitar players really are for the most part a classy, pleasant bunch. Guys like James Burton, Steve, Vince, and Albert all have one thing in common—they are badasses. And yet they are modest about their abilities.

I've attempted to praise Albert on many occasions, and he always deflects the compliment. I guess he really doesn't realize the impact he has on guys like me. But boy, he has left a mark. The way a machine gun would leave a mark. Without Albert Lee, a lot of us might have gone in different directions, but he sent all us twangy country chicken-pickers down a way more interesting path. Albert is one of those building-block musicians who changed the way the instrument was played.

My friend Linda Zandstra knows Albert really well. I was playing the Christmas party for the Academy of Country Music in one of my early years, and she called and said, "You know, Albert Lee is in town, and he'd love to come out and sit in with you if you want."

Before that sentence was even finished, I spit out, "Are you kidding? Of course!" And to my amazement, Albert did come sit in. I barely knew him. Keith Urban was brand-new, too, at the time, and he looked at me and said, "Are you kidding me? Albert Lee is sitting in with us?!" My biggest memory of the night was the two of us practicing guitar in the men's room because it was the only place quiet enough to work out arrangements. Or maybe it was because we were afraid we would actually piss our pants if we tried to play for that audience unprepared. Either way, we had to look like idiots to anyone who actually had to take a leak. That night Keith Urban and I both stood there and played one song after another with the great Albert Lee for the first time. There were some trippy moments in the beginning of this ride, that's for sure. Those early days in my career, when it felt like every note I played would build my reputation as a player, were thrilling to say the least. Especially when I was standing next to my heroes.

I also was heavily influenced by the guitar players in the bands. Guys like Greg Jennings of Restless Heart with his studio chops and his incredibly tasteful approach to pop-country guitar parts really got my attention. For a while I was covering multiple Restless Heart songs in my shows and learning every lick on every track of their records. It was music that kids in my school were hearing on crossover/pop stations. I could play it on my car stereo, and they actually already knew it. It was also so sophisticated sounding, so slick. I think it was around that time that I got really serious about learning to play in the studio. I wanted to be the kind of player that the Restless Heart guys seemed to be: studio cats.

Of course there were the guys in Alabama as well. Jeff Cook and Randy Owen really invented a sound. It's something that's hard to define in a book, but it was somewhere between Waylon Jennings and Lynyrd Skynyrd—all the while being based on country songs. In my days playing the gigs and clubs in the Ohio Valley, there was one surefire way to win a crowd over: play 'em some old Alabama. One of the highlights of my recording career is capturing that magic on the song "Old Alabama." When Randy brought out that old Music Man guitar, Jeff put his signature parts down, and Teddy Gentry added his stamp. I was shocked at the time machine we had created. Of all my successful singles, this would be just about the most satisfying. There is nothing I love more than creativity, collaboration, and the feeling of something unique. Combine that with nostalgia as well, and it's a once-in-a-lifetime musical moment. I really think we accomplished that together.

Other major influences would be the West Coast country styles of the Eagles and Clarence White. I have always felt like the music that best exemplified my style was California country, be it Bakersfield or otherwise. I guess I could have packed my bags and headed there. But it was a long drive. That steel-guitar-soaked B-Bender music painted a picture of a desert almost better than Bob Ross on PBS could have. Bernie Leadon, Clarence, Joe Walsh, Don Felder, these guys were all smoking the same stuff. And that's not just a metaphor.

The guitar music of the Beatles, with its heavy rockabilly influence, also spoke to me. It would later be mostly their inventiveness in the studio and their tones and sounds that got me hooked.

But if I had to pick just one player whose style hit me the hardest and shaped me the most, I'd say that it was John Jorgenson and his playing with the Desert Rose Band. (Speaking of California.) I mentioned this band earlier in the book, and I don't even know how to describe how John's guitar sound spoke to me. It was the eighties, and everyone was playing a whole refrigerator rack full of processed gear that sounded more like Toto than Roy Nichols. I love Toto, too, but back then in country everyone put delay and compression all over their guitar parts. It seemed to go against the simplicity and earthiness that country music was claiming to champion. People'd be singing about Kentucky, but it sounded like New York. And then along comes the Desert Rose Band out of California, and they're using heavy pedal steel and a bluegrass rhythm style with Herb Pedersen and the singing of Chris Hillman, who was a key member of the Byrds and the Flying Burrito Brothers. They had all the balls of those old Emmylou Harris records. Wait, what? Anyway . . .

To top it all off, on lead guitar there's John Jorgensen, and he's one of the most insanely talented guitar players we've ever had in country music.

When the Desert Rose Band came through the Wheeling Jamboree, they blew my mind, and in a way I'm still not over it. I can remember watching John plug a Telecaster-style guitar right into a delay pedal and into an old Vox AC30, which had never previously been used in country music. That was the kind of amp used for Beatles records, Led Zeppelin, etc. So John Jorgenson took what Don Rich did and added this British Invasion thing and his own meaty, melodic, nimble style. Instantly, as if given a mission from God, I thought, *I'm getting one of those amps and I'm learning to play as close to this guy as I possibly, humanly can.* Because the way John plays is otherworldly good.

This was one of those many moments when being a part of the Wheeling Jamboree became my fantasy camp. Not only do I see John Jorgenson play at a young age, I get to open for him, to meet him, and even to have a man-to-boy talk about amplifiers. That's the conversation that got me to make what was the biggest investment of my young life (which I wrote about earlier) and also learn about the premium cost of international phone calls.

If I had to pick just one player whose style hit me the hardest and shaped me the most, I'd say that it was John Jorgenson and his playing with the Desert Rose Band.

After the Desert Rose Band, John went on to play with Elton John and to form an amazingly brilliant group called the Hellecasters. When he left the Desert Rose Band, the guys got back together to play for Buck Owens's seventieth birthday party around the year 2000. John was not able to attend, so they were going to just do it without lead guitar until this new artist with a paisley Telecaster walked up and said, "Hey, I know these songs. I'll play." You should have seen Chris Hillman's face when the solo in "Hello Trouble" came around and I nailed it. He shot me a look that was both flattered by my devotion and sad for my obvious lack of social life during the eighties. Again recently, I lived out one of my dreams when I got to sit in with the Desert Rose Band for a reunion show they did in Nashville. I played on "Hello Trouble" again, but this time with John and I each trading solos and then doing harmony parts. And fantasy camp continues.

I actually got to play with Chris Hillman a few more times, one of them when we came together to honor Buck Owens. Shortly after Buck died in 2006, I was invited to participate in a tribute to Buck at the Academy of Country Music Awards in Las Vegas. The band for our tribute that night featured Dwight Yoakam, Billy Gibbons from ZZ Top, original Buckaroos steel guitarist Tom Brumley, Buck and Bonnie Owens's son Buddy Alan Owens, and Travis Barker of Blink-182 on drums.

I'll never forget that afterward, Chris Hillman took me aside and said, "I want to tell you something. When I was in your shoes, I was an asshole. Brad, I've been watching you closely these past few days, and I am happy to say, you are so far from an asshole. I am *so* proud of you. Keep your head on your shoulders, and don't mess it up."

This was honestly one of the nicest things that anyone had ever said to me, especially while using the word "asshole."

Guitar Tips from Brad

LESSON # 5

Play what you know. Or at least what you *should* know.

6

THE WORLD

You think you're one of millions
But you're one in a million to me.

—"The World,"
written by Brad Paisley, Kelley Lovelace, and Lee Thomas Miller

I think back to that kid soaking up every note in Wheeling, West Virginia. What a rich foundation playing live radio on the Jamboree had given me. I could play a show on a major stage on Saturday night, record it, go home, and listen to it, and I could hear where I'd nailed it and where I'd blown it. I certainly had a leg up on anyone living in a music-starved town. But now, I was growing up. The days of being the cute teenager who played for old folks were coming to an end. So much was waiting down the road. A bold new world beckoned. I wanted to see what I could achieve, go for it all, give it everything I had. There's a time and a place for everything. It's called college.

I've witnessed quite a bit in my time, but here's something that I've never seen: a popular musician runs up onstage to accept a big prize at a fancy award show, only to have security stop him at the steps and ask, "Sir, can we see your diploma, please?" I've also never seen Brian O'Connell, my promoter at Live Nation, ask for my GPA when deciding whether or not to book me somewhere. Nor did EMI publishing ask to see my grades before signing me as a writer fresh out of school.

From a fairly early age, I knew in my heart that I was going to do whatever it took to be a guitar player of some sort. In my mind, this meant that whatever degree I eventually earned was most likely not going to determine how well I did in this life. At least that was how I justified to my parents and myself why I let the academic side of my life, um, slide. Instead, I focused almost completely on figuring out the music business. At school, I had always gotten away with doing the exact minimum that I had to do in order to get by. I guess I was smart enough that just attending class was usually adequate for me to retain the information necessary to pass tests. Okay, sometimes I did slightly less than that.

Still, as the proud son of a schoolteacher, I understood on some core level the value of getting a formal education. And I made a promise to my bookworm mom that I would get a college diploma. So after graduating from John Marshall High School, I took my tattered academic record and went to West Liberty State College—now known as West Liberty University—in Wheeling, West Virginia, for two years. While I was there, I learned that if I ever wanted to make it in music—and *boy*, did I ever want to make it—then possibly going to Belmont University in Nashville would be my best bet. For one thing they had a great music business program. For another, they were actually in Nashville. More specifically, right at the end of Music Row.

As it turns out, there is no easy or even direct path to making a name for yourself in the music world. If there was, I've got a feeling that would be one busy path with incredible traffic and people trying to knock you over all along the way. However, I had personally spoken with and asked advice from many people already working in Nashville, and time and time again, I heard that Belmont University was the sort of place where you could get plugged into some of the circles that might help you establish yourself in Music City, USA.

Until this point, I had not done a whole lot of serious thinking about how to get where I wanted to go. Now, perhaps for the first time, I began to ponder life and how I was going to get the privilege of spending mine making music for a living. I figured that one of my best shots might be to get to Nashville while I was still in college. That way I could take chances before some of those big, bad pressures of real life hit me and I suddenly had a mortgage to pay, a family to support, or any other actual grown-up responsibilities to consider.

Applying to Belmont University turned out to be among the best and most important decisions of my entire life. From the second that I started playing music, I dreamed of someday actually living in Nashville. And right from the very first night that I spent there after I enrolled, Nashville felt like home. And it has ever since.

Before attending Belmont, I had only been able to make the pilgrimage to Nashville a couple of times. A few trips here and there, some for business, some for fun, and I really felt the pull of this place like a paper clip to a high-powered magnet. I remember attending Fan Fair as a fan, watching the stars sign autographs in their booths and then perform at the grandstands.

As it turns out, there is no easy or even direct path to making a name for yourself in the music world.

I still remember standing there in the crowd, looking at that stage, and feeling like the distance from the audience to the spotlight was a good thousand miles.

Arriving at Belmont, I felt instantly welcomed by my fellow students—many of whom were there for the same basic reasons I'd come. Belmont students are a unique lot. It's not a cutthroat music school. It's a Southern Baptist university. And it's the South. That means there's a decency and warmth in all things. Competition is fierce but has a "Bless your little heart" attached. And there's room for everybody. Though I did not know it yet, among the students at Belmont were a number of people who would eventually figure prominently in my music life—including the kid who would become my future producer, a label executive or two, one of my main songwriting partners, my fiddle player, and some of my closest friends.

It didn't take long for me to fall head over heels in love with this crazy artistic Southern town. How could a guy like me resist? Within my first forty-eight hours in Music City, I hit the streets. I drove over to a meeting at Opryland Theme Park with one of my few contacts. I had already auditioned long-distance to try to get a gig as a musician and performer there. The same company had previously offered me a gig at Gaylord Texan Hotel, but Texas wasn't where I needed to go. So I passed on it but kept the numbers of the people who had believed in me. So I figured that just as soon as I hit town, I'd stop by Opryland and pay a visit to tell the powers that be that

I was around. I was hoping that by some chance they'd need another guitar player at the now-defunct theme park. Certainly they'd need me, right? Because guitar players in Nashville are as rare as blades of grass. So I set out to pay a visit to a guy I'll call Matt (because I can't remember his name) who hired players for the theme park.

Well, as it turned out, the offices for the Opryland Park were right there at the Opry House itself. So when I arrived at the Opry backstage door, I thought, *It can't be this easy!* And I walked right in. At this point, I was already completely taken aback because I could not believe I was roaming around freely backstage at the Opry. True to form, I was so excited that I got a little lost. I looked around for someone to ask directions. No one. So I ducked my head into one of the Opry offices to ask for a little help finding my way in this new place. And there before me, larger than life, was Porter Wagoner—but not in his typical rhinestones; instead, he had on a camo fishing cap and jeans. But it was Porter Wagoner just the same. What on earth could I possibly say to such a distinguished and truly iconic figure in country music history?

"Um, hey, Porter, do you know where I can find Matt So-n-so?"

This being country music, Porter Wagoner could not

have been nicer, and he informed me that I could find Matt by going across the parking lot to the white building. I said, "Thanks, Porter. See you later"—six years later, actually.

As soon as you arrive in Nashville, you realize that it is called the "Athens of the South" for a reason. Nashville is an incredibly artistic town right in the middle of the Bible Belt. It's a big, beautiful contradiction. It's like a rock star in a church pew. It's the Bible-publishing capital of the world, and at the same time, it's the place Harlan Howard wrote the book on cheatin' songs. The two need not be mutually exclusive. I find it to be the healthiest of combinations—it offers the old moralistic virtues of the South along with the freethinking creativity of all the modern artistic movements.

Unlike some other places where people go for the business of music, it's also a very real and very human place. There is an accountability in Nashville. In New York or L.A. you can be a complete prick. It won't matter. You couldn't possibly offend enough people to make a dent in the population wide enough to affect your job or reputation. It's just too big. It's not even real. It's massive and make-believe in those places. In

Nashville you have to work together on these few streets that make up Music Row, because you will see your nemesis at the Pie Wagon at lunch. Screw somebody over and mark my words, they will be two tables over at South Street at dinner. Or at the very least, across the room at the Pancake Pantry the next morning. And eventually we will make you leave and go to one of those bigger places where you belong.

There's an openness here though, too. For me, the true spirit of Nashville and country music is best captured in something that the great songwriter Harlan Howard once said (and that helped inspire my song "This Is Country Music"). Once, somebody was giving Harlan a little grief about one of his cheating songs, specifically about whether he was glorifying infidelity by writing it. Harlan wasn't having any of that. "No, I write songs about things people do," Harlan told them, "whether they're right or wrong."

That's country music—that simple but wonderful idea of just telling the truth. It's at the heart of what the best writers do so well here in Nashville. Country music is sort of like reality radio—as opposed to reality TV, where it seems they just make the stuff up. Nashville is a town that excels at giving people a powerful platform to tell the truth for mass consumption. This *truth* is the secret weapon in country music.

The art of our town comes from painting an honest picture in living color.

And there's another thing that I've always loved about Nashville: our town is different from other entertainment capitals of the world because there's an unspoken (and occasionally spoken) rule here—no matter who you are, or how big you get, you can't forget where you came from. If Porter Wagoner can be nice to a fool like me backstage at the Opry, then who am I to be anything other than nice as well? This is a country tradition that other genres of music could learn from a little. Roy Acuff wasn't a jerk, and Little Jimmy Dickens is maybe the nicest guy in the world. These people *created* country music, so who are any of us who follow in their footsteps to act like idiots and treat people badly? It is my belief that the precedent has been set. No changing it now.

At Belmont, I wasn't trying to walk in anyone's footsteps yet—I was just trying to get my foot in the door. I took whatever courses were required and for once in my life, I actually paid some attention. The degree that I was there to get wasn't even technically in music; my degree was in music business—

which is actually a bachelor of business administration degree. So I actually put my college education straight to work for me and had it pay off right away. I still remember every word and statistic I learned in publishing class about the statutory royalty rates and how publishing can be split in different ways. I vividly remember hearing from one of my professors about what writing a number one song might possibly earn you. It was eye-opening, and almost every bit of it ended up being highly relevant to my life. I devoured it. I even went to the bookstore and bought the books for all my classes. A first for me.

My academic record, sadly, is not without one painful yet hilarious blemish. What I am about to tell you is not something that I'm proud of, but I believe that you good people reading this trash have a right to know. First, please take any small, impressionable, guitar-playing children safely out of the room.

> *I even went to the bookstore and bought the books for all my classes. A first for me.*

Okay, I have a horrible confession to make here among friends.

I, Brad Paisley, future multiple winner of the *Guitar Player* magazine reader's poll for best country guitarist . . . got a D in guitar.

What the hell, right? Well, I can explain . . .

It was my first semester at Belmont and the class was taught by a great jazz player named Marty Crum who still plays around Nashville.

At the same time, I was pursuing several opportunities in town, including a number of internships and a few females, and so I may have skipped my guitar classes a few times that first semester. Okay, maybe I skipped a few times more than a few times. Stupidly, I figured that I could clearly play guitar, so how bad a grade could I get?

I found out about my grade when I went home to West Virginia, right in time for my parents to receive my first report card from Belmont—the one in which I got a D in guitar. My parents hit the ceiling. I still recall my father yelling at me—and he hardly ever yelled, unless I *really* deserved it. "Of all the *damned* things for you to fail at—a D in *guitar*! You pack up your things and move to Nashville, and the one thing you're there to do— the one thing you're actually good at—you bring home a D!?"

As usual, Dad had a point. So I called up Mr. Crum, over the holiday, and I said, "What can I do about this? I can't have this on my record." And he told me, "What you can do is show up for class, Brad. This grade isn't about your playing. It's about you not even showing up or learning anything that I told you to learn." He had a point too.

"This is going to ruin my academic record and break my parents' hearts. Is there anything that can I do to at least turn this D into a C? Anything. I'm begging you," I said.

"If you come back to school, and learn these things and play them for me, and promise not to miss another class this year, I'll give you a B." And he kept his word.

Now whenever I get a little too cocky—and that can happen—I think back to that D in guitar. And you know who's happiest in retrospect? My parents. They are actually sadistic about it. It is one of their go-to knock-me-down-a-peg weapons. If I'd known how much they were going to love having it to hold over my head, I wouldn't have worked so hard to change it to a B.

SOLO

A day before his seventeenth birthday, Brad's laboratory exploded, giving him a supernatural ability to play guitar but also leaving him hairless. Unbeknownst to most of his fans, Brad is completely bald on top. That's why he wears the hat even to bed.

—JIMMY KIMMEL

Other than in jazz guitar that first semester, I worked diligently during my time at Belmont, especially in my internships. I knew enough to know that I needed to know more. I interned as many places as possible—ASCAP, Fitzgerald Hartley management, and Atlantic Records. I decided I would be discreet at my internships and not be too outspoken about my aspiration to be an artist. I realized that anybody hiring someone for a position, albeit a nonpaying one, didn't want to think the person they're hiring really wanted to be doing something else. I also had just enough sense to realize that just like in any business, I needed to meet the right people, and maybe a few of the wrong people too. I was most excited about that.

My first internship was my best. That was at ASCAP—the American Society of Composers, Authors and Publishers, one of the leading performing rights organizations on earth. I found myself working with John Briggs, an important membership representative, and Connie Bradley, who was the head of ASCAP's Nashville office. There could not have been a better place for me to learn about music publishing and songwriting.

When I first started at ASCAP, I didn't tell anybody I played or wrote. I just absorbed everything going on around me. John Briggs had gone to Belmont himself and had been an intern too, so he knew what I felt like. Early on, John told me, "I'm going to take you *everywhere*." And he did. He took me to every showcase and every board meeting. He had me go as his stenographer to some meetings, even introduced me as his assistant at others. That was the best education I could have ever received. I met people I still see now and who still remember me as John's intern.

Eventually at ASCAP, a few people figured out that I wrote songs—mostly because they started asking me, and I didn't want to lie. One day, Tom Long—another member's rep and great guy—asked me to play him one of my songs in his office, and I said, "That's not why I am here."

Tom replied, "Don't be modest—play me a damn song!"

I said, "I don't—"

"Play me a song or you're fired," he said jokingly. I reminded him I was working there for free. But in the end, how was I to refuse?

I played Tom a song called "Before I Heard Your Name." It was kind of a schmaltzy love song but heartfelt.

Tom heard me sing and play this little number, and he

flipped out. He said, "Play me another." I did. He went and got John Briggs and said, "John, get in here. Have you heard your intern sing yet?" John admitted that he had not. He then proceeded to listen and quickly said he thought I had what it took. After that day, these great people at ASCAP began to unashamedly cultivate my writing ability. They set me up cowriting with some great writers, and they even put me in the coveted songwriter workshop they offered, where top writers like Gary Burr, Pat Alger, Mike Reid, and Tim DuBois would come in, speak, and critique. Looking back now, I know for a fact that the path I wound up taking was due to ASCAP. They would eventually send me to meetings, which led to my first publishing deal at EMI. They allowed me to actually observe the way business was done, as opposed to merely fetch coffee and make copies. And they accidentally introduced me to the most talented song guy I would ever meet—Chris DuBois.

Chris DuBois was roughly my age, had just graduated, and got hired as a new-membership rep at ASCAP about three months after I started my internship. Our similar sense of humor was obvious right away, and we really hit it off. When he found out I wrote songs, he wanted to hear them. So I would frequently go into his office and play him what I was working on. His advice was always amazing; he really had a knack for knowing the best way to make a song better. One time, I went in with a half-done song, and he had a hundred suggestions on how to improve it. I said, "Why don't you just write it with me?" He said, "Hmm. All right. Maybe I could." And just like that we sat down after work and began the first composition of what would be a hugely successful songwriting team. The amazing thing is, Chris had never even tried to write a song prior to that night. Years later he would win the ASCAP country songwriter of the year award.

Next I interned for Atlantic Records. I interned in record promotion and worked with a woman named Debbie Bellin, who was an excellent promoter. It was all part of my plan to try to cover every aspect of the business. The way I saw it, I couldn't believe they were going to let me walk into a record company like Atlantic Records every day (free of charge) and watch what a record company does. Why wouldn't you do that if you want to be in the music business?

I remember driving around these buildings on Music Row when I first arrived in Nashville and thinking, *What's going on in there? Is Alan Jackson inside there right now recording some hit song? Is Joe Galante planning the launch of the next big band?* I have a feeling that today people walk into record company buildings asking, "Can I see Brad Paisley, please? Where do you keep him?"

Finally, there was my most bizarre internship—with the very successful management company Fitzgerald Hartley. This was my only bad experience as an intern. It just wasn't a good situation, and I didn't feel needed and didn't really learn anything. They had nothing for me to do, and I wasn't invited to any events—I didn't get any respect from the other interns who had been working there for years. I basically just moved paper from one folder to the next. I even quit two weeks early. I left that internship having learned only one thing—that these Fitzgerald Hartley people would never *ever* get to manage me.

Fast-forward to now. Bill, Larry, and Mark at Fitzgerald Hartley have been managing me since 2003. Oh well. Never mind.

At Belmont, during those years, I was really known as a guitarist. I lived and breathed the instrument. I briefly worked at Corner Music in Nashville, stringing and selling guitars, and I played every session I could. I befriended some engineers and pro-

I couldn't believe they were going to let me walk into a record company like Atlantic Records every day (free of charge) and watch what a record company does.

ducers at school, like Frank Rogers, who would later produce me, and a great kid named Doug Sadler, who was into
learning studio engineering as much as I was studio guitar. I
was fascinated by the process of getting guitar on tape. That
magical cauldron that took these temporary vibrations out
of thin air and captured them forever on a disc. From the
Beatles to Buck Owens, I wanted to do that very thing. Make
some sounds that would live on, be unique, and be me.

The great thing about school was the studio. Open to
students between the hours of seven thirty A.M. and ten P.M.
Well, in theory. If you're creative, and if I'm anything I'm creative, you could get away with much more.

Because Doug was a studio student adviser, he had the
keys. So we would book the last session of the day, the evening. This meant that when a teacher came by at the end they
would just see Doug and say, "Hey, lock up, will ya?"

"Sure thing," Doug would say, "about done." We weren't.
We were just getting started.

We would work all night. We'd record guitar, bass, piano
tracks; then we'd listen down and usually try it again. Over
and over, trying to beat what we had and find some magic.
I would have my old AC30s in a booth, trying tone settings,
and Frank would bring in an acoustic, and we'd mess with

mics. By sunrise, when we could barely keep our eyes open any longer, we'd start packing up. We needed to be outta there before faculty came in.

I remember one day the dean, Bob Malloy, came around the corner of the storage room at seven A.M. or so as we were putting the last of the speakers away. We stopped dead in our tracks, one guy on each side of these amp cabinets, halfway through the door of the storage room, thinking, *Oh shit! We're caught.* But in a moment of brilliance, we started backing out with the cabinets like we were setting up for a session. Bob took one look and said, "You boys sure are off to an early start today. Good job! The early bird gets the worm, you know."

After I graduated, I heard they installed surveillance cameras in the studio, making that sort of all-nighter impossible. That's too bad. I learned more before seven A.M. than most kids learned all day.

Guitar Tips from Brad
LESSON #6

Don't play just to impress someone. Unless that someone is really hot.

7

WHEN I GET
WHERE I'M GOING

The first thing that I'm gonna do
Is spread my wings and fly.

—"When I Get Where I'm Going,"
written by George Teren and Rivers Rutherford

I hope I don't get hurt patting myself on the back while writing this chapter, but here's where I finally get to go from being some schoolkid who scores the occasional C-note playing guitar and singing a few songs to making the grade as an actual professional and nearly grown-up musician.

This is where I get where I'm going professionally—or at least on the right path.

I made a couple of smart decisions right about now, especially for a guy who'd recently earned that D in guitar. First of all, I didn't rush into any kind of bad deals right away, as people tend to do when they're starting out. Second, thanks to all of those connections I made during my time at Belmont, I suddenly began to feel some real interest from the Nashville music community. Since I had personally interned for a significant portion of that music community, I was pleasantly surprised to find out that some of those people liked me okay. I'm a great believer in watching and waiting for your turn, and it's worked out well for me.

If you remember, I had decided not to tell anyone during my first year at Belmont that I even wrote songs or sang. Just be a player. In more ways than one. Well, really just the one. Still, I played backup guitar for people in the big Belmont Showcase Series and got to know the school. A great girl named Sally Smithwyck had me play lead in her band in several different showcases. So I made a name for myself as the go-to country guitarist in the school. And I was booked solid in that capacity.

In fact, when I was playing for Sally, she really let me shine. She found out I could play fast, so she wrote a fast song that showcased guitar. I really got to burn. It was after one of these really great nights that Frank Rogers came backstage. Even though Frank and I played together in the studio, we didn't take each other very seriously. After I tore that solo up, he said, "You know, I think we should try to record something together sometime." The rest is history.

Finally the next year I was ready to try it myself. I went all-out and entered and won the Belmont Country Showcase.

This earned me a chance to appear in the Best of the Best Showcase, where Belmont presents the winners in various categories and even invites the A & R community to come and see the show.

So I decided to enter the Songwriters Showcase too, but to do so, I needed five good songs. At best, I had three— including one called "Another You" that would ultimately become my first outside cut. (Eventually, "Another You" would go on to become a top-five country record for David Kersh, a man from Humble, Texas, whom I must hereby thank for a number three single, a bass boat, and my first house.)

Back before all that seemed possible, I was still desperately trying to pull together five songs that could showcase what I could really do. The problem was, there weren't five songs that could show what I could do. Just those three or so. And I also realized I had too many ballads and not *any* real up-tempo songs. So I got together one night with my cowriter and future producer Frank Rogers and said to him, "We *really* need a crowd-pleaser here. Something that could lighten the mood and bring the house down." So Frank and I sat down and wrote "I'm Gonna Miss Her"—also known as "The Fishin' Song." I debuted it at the Belmont Songwriters Showcase, and, well, it brought the house down. This little funny song was just about to change my whole life a couple different times in a couple different ways.

Next I performed at a big ASCAP showcase. My adopted family there really never let me go after I finished my internship and was bound and determined to see me achieve my true potential. The showcase went great, and just as I was about to graduate Belmont, EMI Music Publishing came calling. At the time, I convinced myself not to sign anything as a writer until I graduated. I figured I just needed to get through college, keep my promise to my mom, and then I would deal with the rest of my life.

> *This little funny song was just about to change my whole life a couple different times in a couple different ways.*

Fortunately, right after I picked up my diploma from Belmont, Pat Finch from EMI formally offered me my first deal as a professional songwriter. Within a week or so of graduation, I became a professional songwriter making $22,500 a year.

I was twenty-one years old at the time and had learned during college that I could go to Kroger and eat a very balanced diet for sixteen dollars a week, covering both of the two major food groups—macaroni and cheese.

At this point, I worried a lot less about my eating and a lot more about my songwriting. In the back of my mind, I decided that I needed to have a couple of albums of songs written before I ever got a record deal. More than anything, I wanted to be prepared. So I started writing constantly, sometimes on my own and often with the new circle of talented friends that I had started to run with. I began getting together with some combination of Chris DuBois, Frank Rogers, and Kelley Lovelace almost every night. We would write until three or four in the morning, when one of us began to fall asleep in the chair. By the way, the particular chair in my condo that Chris DuBois would usually drift off in was my Papaw's old "Archie Bunker" chair. When I moved to Nashville, I moved it down here with me. And I've still got it. We've completed almost every song we've ever written together with either Chris or I sitting in that thing.

As I look back on it now, those days of all-night songwriting in my little band of brothers were some of the best and most productive of my life. I doubt I could do that sort of thing now, because running wide open in my thirties would probably kill me. Back then we were all young and painfully single, so we were free to get together any night we wanted. We would have loved to have had other plans. We tried like hell to have other plans. But luckily, we usually weren't that lucky.

That shared lack of love in our lives led to a whole lot of songs. I was living outside of Nashville near Brentwood, renting a two-bedroom condo. And as bad as I wanted a more successful dating life, maybe God had other plans. It's hard to write your best songs when you feel no desperation.

Speaking of desperation, I was pretty much a romantic basket case during my early years in Nashville. But let's go back in time . . .

Back when I was still living in West Virginia in 1991 and still going to college at West Liberty, I started dating a girl I'd known in high school. Our first date was going to see a movie she wanted to see called *Father of the Bride* on December 28—I only remember the exact day because that also happens to be my mother's birthday. If you've been living under a rock, the movie starred Steve Martin as the father of

> *As bad as I wanted a more successful dating life, maybe God had other plans. It's hard to write your best songs when you feel no desperation.*

the bride, Diane Keaton as the mother of the bride, and a young actress named Kimberly Williams as, you guessed it, the bride. For my big first date, I took this girl not only to the movies but also to a romantic dinner at Pizza Hut—which in my defense was the second-nicest restaurant in the general vicinity of the Ohio Valley Mall.

As with any young couple, you tend to remember your first-date movies, and I definitely remembered this one. I also remember thinking that the star of the film seemed like the perfect girl. Somehow I felt like this movie had some huge significance in my life. So a year later, when *Father of the Bride* came out on video, we rented it and watched it again to celebrate what was now "our movie." This was definitely what I would consider my first serious relationship. In the context of the guitar, which is what this book is about, this was to be my first real good reason for the thing to gently weep. Or rejoice for that matter. I wrote songs and played gigs with one thought in mind: impressing my girlfriend. I had a muse. I worked construction for her father, and I was around for all the holidays. I was most certainly smitten. It got serious enough that this girl actually transferred to the college I was going to.

Well, not too long after that, my friend Jim "Coach" Watson, athletic director at West Liberty State, convinced me that Belmont was a much better place to go for what I wanted to do. He literally had to sit me down and say, "You belong somewhere else. I don't want you to be one of these guys who has potential and nothing to show for it. And quit thinking about the girl. If it's meant to be, you'll make it. This dream is too big to wait any longer." So after painful deliberation, I enrolled at Belmont and moved to Nashville to follow my dream.

In the first few weeks, the phone calls between the girl back home and the songwriter chasing the dream became less and less frequent. I could tell something was wrong. I was very busy with the business of settling into a new school, but my gut was uneasy. It was one night about two weeks in that my phone rang. It was one of my best friends in West Virginia.

Friend: Hey, are you and _____ still dating?
Me: Yeah, why?
Friend: You might want to make sure she knows that.

And scene.

As it turns out, my being gone was too much for her to take. She ended the relationship in the most final way possible. She started seeing one of my best friends almost immediately.

I was crushed. And I was only twenty. That first real heart-break is a little tough to deal with. I hadn't really allowed for the fact that my new life in Nashville meant the death of our romance. I was thinking about career only. And in that sense, that's what happens when you do that. You are left with career only. Of course, there were much softer ways for her to have ended it. Phone call, letter, long explanation, etc. Betrayal? Well, that's certainly another way to go.

So I spent my first few months in Nashville writing heart-ache songs.

And the guitar would get me through once again. I remember one night when I was at my lowest. I felt alone and down. I was supposed to do a class project where I interviewed a music hero, and weeks prior I had reached out to John Jorgenson. He was living in L.A. at the time and said he'd call if he came to town to record or something but wasn't sure when that would be. So here I am wallowing in self-pity and heartache, at home alone at ten P.M. on a Wednesday, and my phone rings. "Hey, Brad, this is John Jorgenson. I just flew into town to record and wondered if you wanted to do that interview. I know it's late but I figure you're a college kid. Wanna come down to the studio and get that interview done?" So there I was minutes later watching my hero record, in a major

Nashville studio. I was over her for at least a few days after that.

But in retrospect, being a heartbroken guy who was trying to become a country songwriter worked out just fine. That's the thing about a broken heart—it can be prolific. So I wrote more than my share of songs that first little bit. I would set my ex-girlfriend's picture on a desk and literally pretend she was there in person listening. Some songs were sweet and kind, some were more like a Sam Kinison F-bomb screaming routine. Either way, closure was years away.

Two years, in fact. It's December of 1995 and I'm sitting there in my bachelor pad watching TV when a preview comes on for *Father of the Bride Part II*. I remember thinking, *You've got to be kidding me. How do you do a sequel to that? And why now?* This came right at one of those times when I was backsliding emotionally. I'd get over my ex for a while, go out on dates, be fine, and then slowly start to miss her. I'd gone from *I hope she dies* to *I hope she calls*. By now my friends Frank Rogers and Kelley Lovelace had heard just about enough moaning from me. They put it very plainly, as your true buddies will do: I had to get closure with this girl—or I had to get back together with her. One or the other. Then shut the #*!@ up.

This is how I let my buddies talk me into perhaps the single most romantic, pathetic, and foolish plan in the history of bad romance. We decided that I would go to the same theater back home on the same day and time as our very first date and go to see *Father of the Bride Part II*. December 28, just like before. I would be home for Christmas anyway. Our theory was that if this relationship were as big a deal for my ex-girlfriend as it was for me, then she would think of this too. Fate would intervene and we would immediately get back together and live happily ever after. It would be like *Sleepless in Seattle* . . . or rather, in St. Clairsville, Ohio. And if she didn't show up, then I would have closure once and for all, which I needed, and I could finally get on with the rest of my life.

But I am, at heart, a romantic. So I bought into this idea—hook, line, and sinker. On December 28, 1995—while home in West Virginia for the holidays—I got all dressed up and said good-bye to my mom and dad. As I walked out the door, I announced that I was going to the movies.

They asked, "By *yourself*?"

"Yes," I said, and I drove off to the St. Clairsville mall. I even wondered if I should have a long-stem rose ready. But I finally decided that flowers might be a little much. And twice as embarrassing if I was stood up. Stood up? You can't be stood up unless you have a date to start with, dumbass. Anyway, I walked into the theater and bought my ticket for the seven thirty showing of *Father of the Bride Part II*.

As you might imagine, I'm sitting there all by myself in the back and staring at every single person who walks into the theater. Because it was Christmastime and the movie was a big hit, the theater was absolutely packed with people—none of them my old girlfriend. When the previews ended and the movie was about to begin, it was starting to be clear—she was not showing up. Still, I'd already paid for a ticket, so I decided to stay and watch the movie. And even though I had my answer, I still found myself thinking, *Hey, this is a good movie.*

Afterward, I took that long walk out to the car thinking, *That's it; I have closure. Fine. Now it's time to move forward.* But then I realized there was no way that we originally went to

When the previews ended and the movie was about to begin, it was starting to be clear—she was not showing up.

the seven thirty movie on our first date. That would have meant that we had our fancy Pizza Hut dinner at five thirty in the afternoon. So that *had* to mean that our first date had been the late show instead.

So I went back and bought another ticket. This time for the nine-thirty showing of *Father of the Bride Part II.*

Of course my ex didn't show up for that screening either. This time, when the movie started, I could see the writing scrolling up the wall and snuck out.

By this time, my friend Kelley was sitting by the phone waiting for the big news. Once and for all, I was ready to move on with my life. When I got back to Nashville and Kelley and I talked about this humiliating romantic misadventure, I blacked his eye. Kidding. And then we decided that we could at least get a good song out of it. And so we wrote "Part Two," the title track to my second album. I had absolute closure. But that's the thing about closure: it is usually more of a beginning than an ending.

Strangely, I did see the woman I belonged with that evening. Little did I know I was looking right at her.

Failures are funny—you never know when one of them is going to turn into your greatest success.

That's what happened to me when I decided to do a demo of "I'm Gonna Miss Her (The Fishin' Song)"—that funny, crowd-pleasing tune that I wrote with Frank Rogers—at the end of a session, thinking it would be good for a laugh. That same afternoon I got a call that Pat Finch from my publishing company went out with my demo and played it for the famed producer Tony Brown, who wanted our song for George Strait to record. A few hours later, I was informed that there was a little problem—the sort of little problem that you really want to have. Without Pat knowing it, someone else at the company had gone over and pitched the same song to Capitol, and that now Garth Brooks wanted to put a hold on the song. As if that weren't enough good news, we then heard from one of the big A & R men at Arista, Steve Williams, that Alan Jackson wanted to record "I'm Gonna Miss Her" too.

Take a moment to let those three names soak in. I'm just this obscure young songwriter in town with one cut, and suddenly George Strait, Garth Brooks, and Alan Jackson—the three biggest stars in country music at the time, and all of them heroes to me—are interested in my song *in the same day*. That night, putting my recent Belmont education to some proper use, I began to calculate the potential windfall royalty checks that would soon be wending their way toward my mailbox. I had already purchased a newer bass boat, a Corvette, and a much bigger house. In my mind.

Then some reality hit. First, Garth let the song go. Next, George didn't cut it either. Still, Alan had the song on hold for

almost two months, and that was exciting because it was starting to look like he must be serious about it. Finally they let us
know when Alan was going into the studio. With eleven songs
ready, he ended up recording only ten. And the one song that
Alan didn't cut was—you guessed it—"I'm Gonna Miss Her."
When the folks at EMI called me to tell me the bad news, I
probably surprised them. "Then *I'm* going to keep the song
for myself," I said.

That's the moment when Steve Williams at Alan Jackson's
label—the label I most dreamed of recording for—decided to
call up my publisher and ask an excellent question: "So what
other songs does Brad have?" Steve and Mike Dungan (the
vice president and the general manager of Arista) soon got a
tape of some of my songs and in a flash the label became interested in me as more than a songwriter. I remember that Steve
took me to lunch and said, "You know, Brad, I think you're an
artist."

And I said, "You know what? I like the way you think."

Steve said, "Let's explore this." And so we did.

Before long, Arista Nashville was officially interested in
signing me to their roster, and at the same time, RCA was interested too. In the music business as in love, it can be *very*
useful to have at least two suitors because it makes you look

that much more desirable. And who doesn't enjoy a good cat-fight?

We chose Arista, and I believe we made the right choice. Arista proved that when I let them know that I wanted my Belmont collaborator Frank Rogers to produce my first album. They didn't even flinch. Even though neither of us had a lot of what you might call *professional* recording experience (as in absolutely none). But by now I had waited for my moment, and I knew the kind of album I wanted to make, and I believed in Frank and the guys I'd gathered around me. I knew that Frank believed in me, too, and that he would understand that—for instance—I was capable of playing all the guitar on my own album, and that he would not try to make me sound like anyone else.

The team at Arista didn't balk. Instead, they said, "Why don't you guys go cut four songs and let's see how that goes?" So we cut four songs, three of them being "Who Needs Pictures," "Me Neither," and "We Danced." All eventual hit singles, exactly as you hear them on the record to this day. At the same time, I gave the record company a CD with twenty-five songs on it because I'd been stockpiling, waiting for this moment. In that first group of songs were a bunch that would later go on to be hits, like "Wrapped Around," "I'm Gonna Miss Her," and "Part Two"—basically the core of my first two albums. The day he received all of this material, Steve Williams called me up, laughed, and said, "Okay, Brad, why don't we just go ahead and do the box set now?"

What I loved the most about recording that first album was the guitar parts. I had the songs ready, I knew what my voice would sound like, but I got the sense that every guitar part I put on tape was going to define me. I remember those early Desert Rose Band records, where the sound of John's guitar was like an epiphany. I imagined some other kid out there who was going to feel the same way about me. I couldn't let him down, whoever he might be.

Promoting my first single was grueling. I would fly to Portland, Oregon, wake up at 6 A.M., do morning radio shows, and then get on another plane and fly to Seattle. After interviews on drive-time radio shows there, it was back to the airport for the flight to San Francisco. And so on. I did that for almost six months.

I got the sense that every guitar part I put on tape was going to define me.

I have never been so tired. On top of all the exhausting traveling, my first single, "Who Needs Pictures," was struggling on the chart. I remember it being stuck in the forties for almost a month while I was stuck in airports and hotels trying desperately to promote it. I felt like I was spinning my wheels. I seriously wondered if this was the life for me.

I called my friend and promotion rep at Arista, Lori Hartigan, and told her how I was feeling. It was a Sunday night, and I was on my way to the airport to leave again for a week. "I don't think I can do this anymore, Lori. Who am I kidding? I can't take it; I really want to quit."

She said, "You're just tired. You belong on the radio, and you belong in country music. I understand that this is awfully draining. You know what? I think you need a sign. Do me a favor and pray for one. Ask God to show you that you are on the right track. Now, go get on your plane and call me when you land." So I bowed my head and did just that.

I went through security and sat down at the gate. I remember I was going to Phoenix. A girl wearing a Vanderbilt sweatshirt was sitting across from me reading a Bible. We made eye contact, and she said hello. She saw my guitar case.

"What do you do?" she asked.

I told her I was a singer.

"Anything I've heard?"

I said, "Probably not . . . yet." I didn't let on that I was down or struggling. She was on the way to a Bible camp in Arizona. We chatted for just a few minutes and then boarded.

I was halfway through a book and halfway through the flight when someone tapped me on the shoulder. It was the Vandy girl. "I made you a bookmark," she said. She had torn a page out of her Bible, cut it into a rectangle, and wrote, "Philippians 4:13, I can do all things through Him who gives me strength," on the front. I turned it over, and the back said, "Be Encouraged!"

It's funny. It didn't hit me at the time that this was a sign. I thanked her and went back to reading. As I was walking to the baggage claim, my cell phone rang. As soon as I saw Lori's number come up, I realized how blind I must have been.

"Hey, I'm worried about you," Lori said. "I haven't stopped thinking about what you said since you called. Did you get your sign yet?"

"Yeah, Lori, I most definitely did." Then I closed my eyes and thanked God for what was yet another little nudge in the right direction.

The first time I ever heard my record on a car radio, I was in the middle of that promo tour, and I was leaving a radio station in Salt Lake City where I'd just done an interview. I was in the rental car driving back to the airport to head to the next city with my radio rep, and the DJ came on and said, "We had a great guy in here today to play some new songs, and we're going to play a song by him right now. It's brand-new and it's called 'Who Needs Pictures.' This is Brad Paisley." I was completely floored—and I remember thinking, *Boy, my voice sounds weird all sped up like that.*

Thanks to lots of people in country radio, I'd get plenty more chances to hear my voice sped up in the months and years to come. After "Who Needs Pictures," we released the song "He Didn't Have to Be," which I wrote with Kelley Lovelace, inspired by his experiences becoming a stepfather. This was one of those songs that connected with people in a really powerful way. The song moved people the way country songs can do and became my first number one on the country charts. In fact, I believe it was the first number one by a new country artist in a number of years. More than anything, it got the industry's attention from a songwriter standpoint and established me as an artist.

Eventually, "We Danced"—a romantic song I wrote with Chris DuBois about a fantasy of a girl looking for a lost purse in a bar at closing time—gave me my second number one hit. And suddenly, we were off and running. A very big moment for me came in 2000 when I won the Horizon Award at the CMA Awards—sort of country's version of winning Best New Artist at the Grammys. Soon I would be nominated as Best New Artist at the Grammys too—another unbelievable thrill. I have to say that winning the Horizon Award in 2000 was kind of magical—like a big puzzle piece that just fell in perfectly. If I were to have written the script for my life, I might have actually penned it so that I won the Horizon Award in 2000, and then ten years later, in 2010, I'd win Entertainer of the Year. To me, that feels like a healthy climb, so much more satisfying than winning those two awards back-to-back. I've never been about the short run or the quick hit, and I loved the idea of taking my time on this musical journey. I'm pretty sure someone else is writing this particular script, but I'm here to say that I definitely approve of the plot so far.

SOLO

Brad is the consummate modern country guitar hero who combines the influences of the deep classic country pickers with the blues/rock players of the sixties/ seventies rock era. I don't know of anyone who makes playing look so effortless and who loves playing as much as Brad. He is a true musical genius!

—SHERYL CROW

The year I won the Horizon Award, the producers paired up some of the Horizon nominees with more established country stars, and Walter C. Miller—the CMA Awards' executive producer and a big early booster of mine—had the idea of pairing me up with Ricky Skaggs and having me do both the very romantic "We Danced" and the very goofy "Me Neither" to show off the two sides of what I could do. First, I played "We Danced" with my band, and then Ricky came out, played mandolin, and sang with me on "Me Neither." As if that weren't enough, Ricky then stepped forward and announced the winner of the Horizon Award while I stood on the side of the stage. My name was called, and the moment was absolutely perfect—if you can overlook that fuchsia suit I wore that night. One of many questionable wardrobe choices I've made over my career.

Part I of my recording career went like a dream. And as I went on to make my second album, *Part II*—named after the song inspired by the night I saw *Father of the Bride Part II*—I had no idea how poetic things were about to get. I knew the time was right to include a few of the songs I'd held back for just this moment, somehow assuming this sort of moment would actually come. I'm not sure if this was arrogance or stupidity, maybe both, but somehow it all worked out. I remember getting pressure from the label to include "I'm Gonna Miss Her" on my first album. I fought it, believing it was going to be needed as an RBI, to borrow from baseball. In particular, I was convinced that if I had a few hits by now, then a song like "I'm Gonna Miss Her" on the second album could hit it out of the park. I remember Alan Jackson pulling me aside at a party after my first album hit. Alan's a great guy, and I respect him a lot as an artist, so I was glad to have a moment with him. At one point, Alan said, "So are you ever going cut that fishin' song?"

"Yep, it's going on my second album," I said.

"Good. I always liked that song," he said.

"Well, then you should have cut it," I said, kidding him.

But in truth, I may very well owe my recording career, or at least my overall image, to the fact that he didn't. You just never know.

When you first experience success in this world, there is no shortage of ways you can lose your way and screw it all up. We see that all the time, don't we? One of the constants in my life that kept me relatively grounded, and reminded me why I do what I do, has been the Grand Ole Opry. Just as my career was taking off in 1999, I found myself standing on the Opry stage performing for the first time. I was in complete and utter awe. Playing at the Opry makes me feel like a true part of the history of the music that I love. Finding a home there was the fulfillment of not only one of my dreams, but also one of the dreams my grandfather might have had for me.

Warren Jarvis was diagnosed with inoperable pancreatic cancer just a year or so after I started performing with the Wheeling Jamboree. The last time he ever saw me play was when I was opening up for the Judds.

> One of the constants in my life that kept me relatively grounded . . . has been the Grand Ole Opry.

My papaw was in pretty bad shape then and undergoing chemotherapy, but he still came to the show. I dedicated a gospel song to him that night called "His Eye Is on the Sparrow." But what he liked more was the way I rocked out on the guitar covering "Lynda," a really up-tempo Steve Wariner song. I like to think that he left this world knowing that there were great things ahead for me, thanks almost entirely to him. Standing on the Opry stage for the first time, I thought of my grandfather and how much I wished he could have been there with me. In a way, he was with me and always will be.

My experiences at the Opry have changed me forever. It was there that another of my greatest musical heroes became one of my closest friends. I'm talking about the legendary Little Jimmy Dickens. I remember going to the Grand Ole Opry as a new artist, and even though Jimmy couldn't have had any idea who I was, he still treated me with the respect of a colleague and the kindness of a friend. In watching him over the years, I have *never* seen him behave otherwise. Little Jimmy had long been an inspiration to me as a fellow West Virginian who went on to become a country music legend. I was a fan from the first time I saw him from the side of the stage at the Wheeling Jamboree. It was like watching a funny firecracker.

But even before I ever met this man, I could sense his incredibly positive outlook on life and his desire to make people laugh and be happy. Don't let Jimmy Dickens's sense of humor or his relative lack of stature fool you for a second. Little Jimmy is a very big and significant figure in the history of our music. As much as anyone I know, Jimmy has seen it *all*.

This man has been a member of the Grand Ole Opry for more than sixty years and is quite rightly a member of the Country Music Hall of Fame.

Jimmy was there at the birth of so much of what I love in country music. It was the King of Country Music himself, Roy Acuff, who first heard Jimmy on the radio and asked him to come play the Grand Ole Opry. By 1949, Jimmy became a permanent member and went on to be one of the most popular Opry performers ever. Jimmy Dickens was there the night that some new guy named Hank Williams came onstage to play the Opry for the first time. In fact, the story goes that Hank gave Jimmy his nickname "Tater" and even wrote "Hey, Good Lookin' " for Jimmy to record—then, perhaps wisely, decided to save the song for himself.

Back in the fifties and sixties, Jimmy had lots of hits and one of the very best bands around. He had some big crossover smashes, like "May the Bird of Paradise Fly up Your Nose," and some very funny novelty hits, like "A-Sleeping at the Foot of the Bed," "I'm Little but I'm Loud," and "Take an Old Cold Tater (and Wait)." But Jimmy could also break your heart with great tearjerkers like "Life Turned Her That Way" and "(You've Been Quite a Doll) Raggedy Ann"—in fact, he even would hold a Raggedy Ann doll while he sang it. As funny as he is, let there be no doubt that Little Jimmy Dickens has always been one serious talent.

Jimmy Dickens grew up the thirteenth child in a West Virginia farm family, and he was the smallest in his family—the runt of the litter, so to speak. He knew he would never reach even five feet, and that was just the hand that he was dealt. Yet he somehow used what God gave him, or rather withheld, to his advantage. Jimmy played that hand with great heart, great wit, and great success. What other options did he have? As far as I can tell, it was either professional jockey or totally legendary tiny country music singer and comedian. One or the other. He made the right choice.

One night, I went up to Little Jimmy at the Opry and said, "Would you like to go fishing with me someday?" Jimmy said, "Yes, sir." And I said, "Really? Great!" I had always wanted to spend that kind of quality time with this crazy little character. Jimmy asked, "When you wanna go?" I said, "How about Monday morning?" And Jimmy said that sounded fine to him.

I told Jimmy about this pond that my friend Kelley Lovelace's mother-in-law owned about two hours away where we could go catch forty or fifty bass in one day. He said, "Sounds good!" When I called him to confirm our fishing date, he said, "Can't wait, sir!" I told Jimmy that I'd pick him up at seven in the morning that Monday, and he gave me his address and said, "I'll be waiting by the mailbox."

When I called Kelley to tell him that we were going fishing with Jimmy, he said, "Oh man, my in-laws are going to flip," because they are serious Little Jimmy fans. I'm talkin' serious. They're great people who always cooked us a big dinner when we came to fish. Even without diminutive living legends. So we didn't tell them who our new fishing buddy was, just that we were bringing a friend. Here they are in Sand Mountain, Alabama, with absolutely no idea that Little Jimmy Dickens himself is coming to dinner. Finally, it's seven thirty A.M. Monday, and Kelley and I drive by to pick up Jimmy. There the man is with his two fishing poles and tackle box standing at the end of the driveway by the mailbox—looking exactly like a little lawn ornament. Or some sort of Opry garden gnome.

So we drove the two hours down to the pond and had the best time imaginable. We joked and laughed and heard great old stories. Halfway there we stopped at a tobacco shop, where I bought some cigars and also a nice butane lighter that I gave to Jimmy. He still carries it to this day as a memory of our first little trip together. As we pulled up to the property, you should have seen the look on Kelley's in-laws' faces when they saw Little Jimmy Dickens get out of the truck. I thought they were going to cry. Faye, Kelley's mother-in-law, ran inside and started feverishly cooking every favorite recipe she knew of. We fished and ate like fishing and eating were going completely out of style. On the way back home, Jimmy fell asleep in the front seat. He snored all the way back to Brentwood, Tennessee. This was the first day that I ever spent with Jimmy, and it was honestly one of the greatest days of my life. Jimmy's whole philosophy of living has greatly influenced my own. He's become a grandfather figure to my boys, who love him dearly. Recently, I was able to celebrate Jimmy's ninetieth birthday with him, and I've valued every second I've been around this man. I can't get enough of his influence. That may be why I'm always asking him to be in my videos or joking around with him in skits at the CMAs.

I love Little Jimmy Dickens with all my heart and I enjoy every chance I get to stand next to him, and not just because he makes me look taller. All of the on-camera fun that I've had with Jimmy began not long after that first fishing trip, when I asked Jimmy to play my fishing buddy in my video for "I'm Gonna Miss Her (The Fishin' Song)." Our first on-screen adventure together.

So many others became my family at the Opry. Like Bill Anderson, a hero and true class act who I still can't believe I get to pal around with—and just about the best country songwriter of all time. Jeannie Seely, Jim Ed Brown, John Conlee, Porter Wagoner, Connie Smith, Pete Fisher, Steve Buchanan, the list goes on and on. These people became my family. I spent every free weekend at the Opry House when I was new and single. All the stories I would hear backstage, the impromptu jam sessions that would break out in dressing rooms, the lasting friendships . . .

And then there was Johnny Russell. The hilarious larger-than-life Opry stalwart who allowed me into his life in such a big way. We really made a connection. And a year or two after I became a member of the Opry, Johnny would start the decline in health that eventually cost him his life. But I relished our time together. After he had been admitted into hospice care from complications due to diabetes, he lost both his legs. I went to see him around this time, and his sense of humor was still safely intact. I walked in the room, and he was

> *Johnny looked right at me, started to tear up, and said, "I had a ball. I loved life. You make the most of yours too, boy."*

lying back in the bed. He waved me over and whispered very weakly, "Come closer . . . closer . . ." I leaned over and said, "What is it, Johnny . . . ?" He then raised up, grabbed my collar full force, and with complete strength said, "When ya gonna cut one of my songs?!" His family in the room cracked up. That was Johnny.

While I was there, holding his hand, he asked his son John, "Am I dyin'? Be honest." I tried to leave the room and give them privacy, but he held firm and said to stay. John nodded. "Yes, Dad, it won't be long now." Johnny looked right at me, started to tear up, and said, "I had a ball. I loved life. You make the most of yours too, boy."

I walked out of the room and Jeannie Seely was standing in the hall. She said, "Bet you weren't ready for all this when you signed up for this little family. But that's what the Opry is." I said, "I'm ready, Jeannie. I wouldn't trade this for the world."

Years later, after the Nashville flood when I lost all my guitars, John Russell Jr. came out to the farm. He handed me his dad's old Telecaster and a hat he always wore. He said, "Dad would have wanted you to have this. Let's get that collection started again."

LESSON #7

**Don't just read the music. Be the music.
Or write the music—it pays better.**

8

WAITIN' ON A WOMAN

Yeah she'll take her time but I don't mind
Waitin' on a woman

—"Waitin' on a Woman,"
written by Don Sampson and Wynn Varble

When you're talking about something as life-changing as waiting on a woman, you can't rush it. Try as you may, life will unfold around you at its own pace. All you can do is watch the road and wait on the signs.

Around the time I was promoting *Part II*, my second album, little did I know my life was about to become an, um . . . actual life.

Having come through a bunch of less-than-successful relationships in the years since my old girlfriend didn't show up at the movie, it suddenly struck me what I was missing. One morning that fall, either from a dream I'd had the night before that I couldn't remember or just some strange hunch, I woke with the clearest thought: *The person I'm supposed to be with isn't the girl I took to those movies. It's the girl* in *those movies.*

I know it may sound psychotic, but I really had this sense

that this was the woman for me. I really was sure of it. It was that simple.

In concert, I used to share my painful and amusing story of that night I bought tickets twice to *Father of the Bride Part II* before I would play the song "Part Two." I also told the story countless times on air promoting the album. I remembered once talking about it to my friend Peter Tilden on KZLA in Los Angeles when he was doing the morning show and he'd said, "You know, I've met the girl from the movie. She seems like a real sweetheart."

It had been an hour or two since I woke up with the "revelation" of who I should be dating. So I called Peter that morning and said, "You think you could get me in touch with Kimberly Williams from *Father of the Bride*? I'd like to talk to her about being in a video." She could have been a married or divorced chain-smoking crack addict—but as far as I could tell, there was only one way to find out. Being plugged into Hollywood, Peter didn't hesitate. Accepting the challenge, he just said, "Give me ten minutes." Just a few minutes later, the phone rang and it was Kim's manager at the time calling me about this alleged video.

I proceeded to tell this wonderful woman named Tammy Chase the charming story of writing the song "Part Two" and how the *FOTB* movies had influenced my life—intentionally leaving out the part about my being interested in her client for anything other than an appearance in a music video. She was so nice and said, "You know, Kim was just saying she thought it might be fun to be in a music video sometime. Great story! I'll get back to you."

Later, I found out that Kim's manager ended our very pleasant conversation and immediately called Kim. "I just hung up the phone with the greatest guy," she told my future wife. "I just looked him up—he's legit and he's cute. And I know he says he's calling about a video, but you're going to date him." Being very reasonable and extremely humble, Kim said to her manager, "Why would you think that?" The manager told Kim, "Trust me, he's interested." And of course I was. Women have us all figured out before we even meet.

She called back before an hour had passed and said, "Kim loved your story. She's going to call you tonight."

So the *very same day* that I had woken up with this epiphany, my phone rang. "Hello? Is this Brad? This is Kim Williams." Now, this could have been awkward, but it wasn't in the least. We talked for an hour. And despite my worst fears, she was not married, divorced, crazy, or a crack addict. I've never known an actress who isn't at least a few of those things.

We talked on the phone almost every day after that first call, and the time was fast approaching when we would need to meet in person. Around that time she began to ask when I could get away and we could meet and go to dinner in L.A. *Hollywood Squares* made me an offer to come out and film a few shows, so I decided to take them up on a free trip from Nashville to L.A. This was the perfect excuse to get to Los Angeles, where Kim was filming the sitcom she was on at the time, *According to Jim*.

So I boarded a plane and went off into the great unknown. We went out the first night and it went fine, but I had one more night free while I was there. So we got back together for a second dinner. On that second night, I was scheduled to go on *After MidNite,* a syndicated late-night radio show hosted by a great guy named Blair Garner. So I invited Kim to come along with me and hang out. On that night, she got to see me do what I do best. Which is definitely not dinner conversation. She watched as I sat in front of a microphone with my secret weapon, my equivalent of the magic Green Lantern superpowers ring: my guitar. And

So the very same day that I had woken up with this epiphany, my phone rang. "Hello? Is this Brad? This is Kim Williams."

the only prayer I ever had of winning her heart—anyone's heart, for that matter.

So as we began to date, in keeping with the guise of why I called her in the first place, I figured I needed to have Kim appear in a music video.

The "I'm Gonna Miss Her" video was a great way to break the ice together because not only was it fun, but she also became part of something that was an important turning point in my career. A change of direction that was much needed for me.

In this case, the first step toward this turning point was getting my record company to release the song as a single in the first place. Even though this was the same song that helped get me a recording deal, there was some serious resistance at my record company against putting the song out as a single. When I went to Arista to discuss this matter, I was already ticked off because of a recent mishap—I'd recorded a song called "Too Country" with George Jones, Buck Owens, and Bill Anderson that won the CMA Award for Musical Event, and I think it could very well have won a Grammy too. The only problem was someone at the label forgot to submit our record for Grammy consideration. And songs have to be submitted in a certain manner to qualify. So that was that. Pretty embarrassing for my label, and I was furious—not so much for myself but for the genuine country legends on the track; I really wanted to help those guys get a Grammy, which most of them had never won.

So I went into my label with a little attitude that day, and my righteous rage allowed me to sit there with Joe Galante and say, "Well, I think you're about to make another mistake and release the wrong song next." I wanted "I'm Gonna Miss Her" out, but the company was worried that the song was going to offend women. I think they figured they had a pretty good thing going by then with me singing nice, romantic ballads, and they didn't want to risk upsetting the apple cart.

Sometimes I only *think* I know better, but this time I actually knew it in my bones. I'd been playing "I'm Gonna Miss Her" live, and I knew the song was a road-tested crowd favorite with men *and* women. It had never failed to bring the house down. This was one of those times in a music career when you're not just pushing for a single; you're ultimately pushing for a little freedom to be yourself and to let people know who you are in a more honest way. Even though I was on a bit of a roll on country radio, I felt the need to show the world I was not just another guy with a hat and a few romantic hits—that I had a personality and possibly even a functioning sense of humor. Lord knows getting a laugh or two never held back my heroes, like Little Jimmy Dickens, Buck Owens, and Vince Gill.

Perhaps wisely, I didn't try to argue that point. What I said to my record company was "I'm Gonna Miss Her" would sell well for a very basic reason—people responded to it. To close the deal, I went off the cuff and pitched my crazy concept for a video for the song. Imagine, I told them, Dan Patrick as the sportscaster officiating the fishing tournament, and me as a guy whose significant other didn't want him to go fishing with his band and a bunch of other fishing buddies, like Little Jimmy Dickens. And then to represent all sides, we would go on *The Jerry Springer Show* with Jerry Springer in the video playing himself—and a big battle of the sexes would ensue about this very important issue. The big boss, Joe Galante—now the most powerful man on Music Row—took this idea all in and said, "Can you really pull that all off?" I told Joe, "I think so"—even though I hadn't ever even spoken to any of these people. He said, "Okay. We believe in you. Make it happen."

So I hit the phones and started to call upon the kindness of strangers. I asked my agent, Rob Beckham at William Morris, to get a number for Dan Patrick, who I knew had said a few nice things about me on his radio show. When I got ahold of Dan, he said he was in. Next I called Jerry Springer. I think I caught Jerry in the middle of a show taping, but he couldn't have been nicer and told me he was a country music fan. And of course, there was no woman I wanted to abuse me on camera more than Kim.

The next thing I knew, this whole crazy gang was coming together to make this video, and thankfully, it became absolutely everything I dreamed it would be. With a lot of help from that video, "I'm Gonna Miss Her (The Fishin' Song)"— the third single from *Part II*—took my album and shot it way up the charts. The single went to number one for two weeks in a row, turned the album into a much bigger hit, and gave my fans the first large-scale glimpse at that other side of my personality. The success of "I'm Gonna Miss Her (The Fishin' Song)" gave me a lifetime fishing license to just be myself.

One day when it was clear the song was a smash, the head of promotion for Arista Nashville, a great man named Bobby Kraig, who had strongly resisted releasing it as a single, phoned me. "Brad," he said, "I've never been more surprised and happy to be wrong. This one is going down as one of my favorite achievements." Trust me, I was happier than he was. Somehow the very same goofy fishing song that helped me land my record deal had come back into my life and helped me regain my creative freedom.

By now, the team that had helped me make my first two albums had gone from wannabe writers, players, and producers to full-blown pros. So when I began work on my third album, I used the same cast of characters who'd helped me get this far. For the first time, I felt like I could focus on the ground I wanted to cover. "Mud on the Tires"—which I wrote with Chris DuBois—set the tone for the whole third album: more earthy, rootsy, and even outdoorsy. Some of the songs were written while I was dating Kim, like "Little Moments," another one I wrote with Chris. I remember playing Kim the song over the phone while we were dating long-distance and the effect it had on her. Things were really clicking.

My music started feeling more grounded in the reality of life. There are so many songs I love on *Mud on the Tires*. My favorite might be "Celebrity," because it started me down a path of not being limited to traditional country themes. It was my first attempt at depicting the world outside of country music, all the while keeping the style of country. Up until then, I had sung about fishing and dating and family—the sorts of subjects that lend themselves to country music so easily. Now I began to think—what if I wrote a country song about the whole insane pop culture phenomenon that was becoming more and more a part of my life? It turned out to be a major turning point because it opened up my world as a songwriter and as an artist.

The fact that "Celebrity" did so well gave me the license to write about anything I saw around me and still have it feel like a real country song. That opened things up so that I could write "Alcohol" and "Online" and "Ticks" and so many other songs that would follow. I felt I could say what I wanted to say and even nudge the listener in the ribs a little bit.

I think my fans began to get a sense that I'm not just a guy picking songs to be my next hit—that these songs are more meaningful than that to me. Hit songs are great, but now I felt like I'd opened up the lines of communication and could actually comment on life and this world we share. And people were listening. The fact that country music fans and country music radio gave me that freedom meant the world to me.

To all the younger artists out there, here's what I've learned: Define yourself instead of allowing others to do that important job for you. Don't let anybody paint you into a corner or tell you who you are. You tell them.

Something that always astounds me is the way a simple three-minute song, written in a matter of hours, can become a living breathing monster all its own. Songwriters are the ultimate Dr. Frankensteins. We put very little by way of electricity or sweat into actual songwriting, and the next thing you know, studios are booked, albums are being pressed, video locations are being prepped, and people are employed. I'll never forget driving up to the set of the "Celebrity" video. Here's Jason Alexander in the makeup chair, Little Jimmy Dickens has

> *Hit songs are great, but now I felt like I'd opened up the lines of communication and could actually comment on life.*

flown out to appear with the Bachelorette Trista Rehn, and William Shatner is pulling into the parking lot. This was a big deal to me because beyond being a lifelong music lover, I'm also a true American child of television. And you can imagine what it is like to see your song depicted by legendary screen actors. I was having more fun than anyone should ever be allowed to have.

Mud on the Tires also marked the debut of the Kung Pao Buckaroos, an old-timey audio comedy troupe featuring three Country Music Hall of Famers and some of the funniest guys I know—Little Jimmy Dickens, "Whispering Bill" Anderson, and arguably the greatest country singer ever, George Jones. The Kung Pao Buckaroos appeared on a track called "Spaghetti Western Swing," which also featured a musician who had in recent years become another of my favorite guitar players, Redd Volkaert. Redd made a name for himself playing pure honky-tonk swing in the clubs on Broadway in Nashville. The man's an absolute monster player, and soon all the other players in town, like Brent Mason, Vince Gill, and I, would go check him out any chance we got. Eventually, Redd went on tour with Merle Haggard himself, then decided to move to Austin, Texas, where he could play live music to his heart's content. He has shaped my playing in recent years more than any other player. I love what he does so much that when I had the chance to play talent booker instead of talent, I offered him a gig that I hoped would be a once-in-a-lifetime chance: playing my wedding reception.

Kim and I got married out in California in the chapel at Pepperdine University overlooking the Pacific Ocean in Malibu. We got hitched in California because Kim was still filming *According to Jim,* and all of her friends were out there. And of course, her friends are more important than mine. Take note, future grooms.

Kim and I pulled off a unique trick with our wedding. We invited our families and our close friends to the rehearsal dinner—about fifty people—and stressed that we really wanted to share that special time with them before the next day, when there would be a big reception with 250 people or so and a honky-tonk band complete with plenty of Telecaster twang. So there we all were, gathered together in the church, and the wedding planner started telling everybody, "Okay, here's how it's going to happen tomorrow. Brad, you spit out your gum and stand here, and Kim, you come on down the aisle."

Kim came down the aisle with a coat on and a veil over her face. Now all our families and friends are milling around and half paying attention when suddenly Kim takes off her coat and reveals that she's wearing a wedding dress. In an instant, everybody's eyes opened wide. Suddenly they knew why we'd insisted they be at rehearsal. This was no rehearsal—this was the main event.

It was the greatest way imaginable for the two of us to get married. First of all, Kim was in one of the best wedding movies of all time, so how are you going to compete with that in your own life? Secondly, I personally am not a fan of the pomp and circumstance that surrounds most weddings. In fact I hate weddings more than almost any organized event, I really do. As a kid I was always booked singing at weddings and receptions. And perfectly sane people lose their minds, almost without fail, at these "blessed" occasions. "Stand here, wear this flower, no, this flower, did you learn the words? Can you change the words? Not too loud, wait on the cue when they release the doves, can you sing it in a higher key? Would you mind not eating at the reception? We're running a little low on ravioli." No, thank you. I'll pass and send a gift.

Clearly I have issues.

The best part of surprising everyone with our day-early ceremony was it didn't allow the usual suspects to get to full-blown meltdown mode. The next thing they knew, it was too late to get nervous or crazy. The deed had been done.

Since we had this tent on a nice hill overlooking the Pacific Ocean—and a whole bunch of Hollywood people coming—I figured these Hollywood types needed a dose of hillbilly. I remember calling Redd Volkaert in Austin and inviting him and his band to fly in and play our wedding party. And since my own band and I had been on tour until about a week before the wedding, we were about to route everyone so that these guys I love could share our big day too. Everybody got up and played, and we had a massive Malibu wedding-day honky-tonk jam session in that tent. To me, our wedding was the perfect blend of our two separate lives coming together—Kim and all her great Hollywood friends dancing their hearts out to "Crazy Arms."

The next few years were a big, beautiful blur.

More hit singles, and life went pretty well with one large exception: the death of my beloved aunt Rita. This woman was my mother's sister, mom to my cousins Christy and Lisa, and like a second mom to me. She was my mother's best friend, as well. She lost a long battle with cancer. *Lost* is the wrong word. I prefer to see even the end of her life as a victory. This was a woman who fought cancer for seven years when the outlook was nowhere near that optimistic.

The night she died was a Sunday. I remember sitting down to eat and getting the call from my mom, who was with my aunt Rita when she passed. Kim and I had just recently moved onto our farm and had been sending pictures of it back for her to see. Aunt Rita had really hoped to visit someday if she got better. As I heard that she'd taken her last breath, I pictured her floating up and away, much like the accounts of people who've had near-death experiences. Higher and higher, away from her house and her town, free of the prison that a cancer-stricken body becomes. And then, I imagined, she must have headed south to Tennessee, to finally fly over our farm and see it once and for all. I lost it.

In my moment of grief, I suddenly remembered a song my friend Rivers Rutherford had pitched to me that he'd written with George Teren—"When I Get Where I'm Going." That song was exactly my wishes, my take on the departure and destination of my aunt's soul. I tried to recite the words to Kim but couldn't keep my composure. I had to cut it. No finer lyric has ever been written that so perfectly expresses my own wishes for what happens to us when we die. And I knew that song would be life-changing for a lot of people after they got a chance to soak in the message of it. That is the power of a great country song. To be your life in a song. Or in this case, even the end of your life. It also didn't hurt the emotional impact of the song that I enlisted a "little ole" singer from East

Tennessee named Dolly to harmonize with me on it. I am still so proud of that moment in my career and what it has meant to other people. Country music is important, sometimes, I think. Correction. I know it is.

At Rita's funeral, I got up to speak. I don't know how I ever made an audible sound. I have never been that emotional—whether it be at an award show, wedding, or otherwise. But no one from our family felt like they could do it, so that left me. Mr. Get-up-in-front-of-people—I'm so glad I did. I think I discovered something in that moment.

That is the power of a great country song. To be your life in a song.

One thing I got to say that day, which has stuck with me, was about *fear*. Life is about conquering it. No doubt about it. I believe one thing we are all here to do is learn how to overcome our fears and doubts, whatever they may be. Learn how to beat the things that keep us down. My aunt did that. She fought cancer valiantly and without much scientific encouragement. She lasted seven years when she was not supposed to last three. In that time she saw her youngest daughter get married. She saw the birth of Emily, her first granddaughter. She watched her hair fall out, bought wigs, and went on. She got to go to my wedding. She faced fear, faced the knowledge that she was on borrowed time, and made the most of it. It doesn't mean she didn't feel fear; she just wasn't at the mercy of it.

At the funeral, about a thousand people showed up to say good-bye. They filed past, one by one, in the family greeting line. I remember looking at Kim, who had only been married to me for less than a year at that point, standing there gracefully greeting people, representing our family for the first time in grief. And I remember knowing I'd married the right woman and that all of us would never be the same after having experienced this. I for one was inspired, and I still am.

My aunt Rita loved the rain. In the summertime, she would go for walks in it, and she always talked about how she loved a great downpour. Well, when I was recording the vocal for "When I Get Where I'm Going," it was a cloudless day. Blue sky, as far as I could see, as I drove to the studio. No chance of rain. Well, what do you think happened as I started to sing—right out of the clear, blue sky?

I thought, *Hi, Aunt Rita. Hope you like the song.*

Some Native Americans thought dancing could make it rain. I don't know about that. But boy, music sure can.

I love looking back at the things that seem meant to be. Divinely guided. I have so many examples, musically speaking and otherwise. One of those miracles, which I'm so thankful for, was on its way via North Carolina.

I'd always said there was only one actor who could perfectly bring to life the main character in the song this chapter is named after. So I asked Andy Griffith to star in the video for "Waitin' on a Woman," directed by Peter Tilden and Jim Shea. We were very lucky that Andy's wife Cindi had heard the song and told Andy, "You've got to do that video." There's a lesson: start with the boss.

As I expected, Andy was amazing in the video, and getting to know Andy Griffith turned out to be another one of those thrills where there were times when I had to pinch myself. Growing up as a small-town guy, *The Andy Griffith Show* was my absolute favorite. Since then, I've been honored to visit Andy many times at his house—and in 2010, I even surprised him and brought the whole band with me to play bluegrass for him in his living room. We gave Andy his own concert while he sang and played along with us. I knew Andy had always said that was his favorite part of the show, having all those amazing musicians, like the Dillards and Clarence White, as guest stars. He loves music more than anyone I know. And getting to be there for him in this way, to give him this gift of music, is as cool as it gets. That's the thing about this guitar my grandfather wanted me to adopt. It really can change lives and brighten days. Even for one of the greatest living icons of our time. Andy created a place we all visit to get away from reality and enjoy the simpler things. And I got to do the same for him that afternoon. If only every small town had as much great music as Mayberry.

William Huckleberry Paisley was born in Nashville, Tennessee. I remember standing at the nurses' station, ballpoint pen in hand, filling out the name certificate. I was thinking, *We really gonna name him this?* I said, "Let the name Huckleberry stand for the power of the pen, the spirit of a freethinker, the adventure of a river winding toward the sea." And soon it would also stand for waking up at two A.M. and four A.M. almost every night.

With so much to celebrate in my life, I decided the time had come to just play. So I once again went to my record company and made what they could well have considered an indecent proposal—making a primarily instrumental album that would possibly confuse country radio and my fans, some of whom were still largely unaware that I played guitar. I was searching for a way to shake things up and live out one of my long-standing musical dreams. This was a labor of love that I had to try.

Before he passed, Buck Owens told me that if I recorded an instrumental album, it could be a big hit. "Man, if you get hot enough, you could take an instrumental to number one," Buck told me. I wasn't so sure about that, but I still wanted to take the opportunity to try something new and have a ball.

Recording the album that I called *Play* was probably the least pressure and most pure fun that I've ever had recording an album. I knew it wasn't going to set any sales records, and that wasn't the point. The whole process of making *Play* was free of all those normal expectations that can keep you second-guessing yourself if you let them. Instead, *Play* became a kind of wild guitar party, and I got to put anyone I wanted on the guest list, from James Burton, to Vince Gill, to Snoop Dogg.

The album was full of instrumentals—like the opening, "Huckleberry Jam," written for my new son, and "Kim," which you might have guessed is for Huck's mom. There were some vocals too. My buddy Keith Urban recorded the duet of "Start a Band" with me. We had a blast through the process, and it became a number one hit for us.

I also flew to Las Vegas and cut "Let the Good Times Roll" with the legendary B. B. King, then just sat around and listened to some of the King of the Blues's great stories. B. B. reminded me a bit of Jimmy Dickens; he's a great man of music whom everybody loves to be around because he has seen it all and has an amazingly positive way of looking at life—especially for a bluesman. Snoop had asked me to play guitar on a song of his, and while I was doing that, I asked him to do a little rap introduction to one of my songs called "Kentucky Jelly." We hit record and Snoop went at it for seven minutes. Rap was a form of music that I never fully appreciated, but then you see a guy like Snoop Dogg, who's the real deal, spontaneously create his own musical monologue—and your appreciation grows. It was amazing—like watching a great jazz musician take a solo.

═══ S O L O ═══

Brad Paisley is a monster *guitar player. He is ridiculously good. We tend to pigeonhole people in music today, and Brad has become such a massive country star that to some people he's just a guy in a cowboy hat who writes and sings all these great songs. But Brad is also an amazing musician who could hold his own in any town playing any kind of music. As I judge him, Brad Paisley is one world-class* dawg.

—RANDY JACKSON

The album gave me a chance to tip the hat to some of the people whose inspiration has gotten me this far. For example, *Play* featured "More Than Just This Song," the song that Steve Wariner and I had written and recorded for our beloved guitar teachers Chet Atkins and Hank Goddard. I also did something magical and once-in-a-lifetime by taking the demo of the song "Come on In"—something new that Buck Owens wrote and recorded in his office—and turning it into a duet for the two of us. Including Buck on the *Play* album also gave me one more chance to pay my respects to the legacy of Telecaster history that Buck almost single-handedly ushered in.

Finally, there is a little number called "Cluster Pluck" that in less than four minutes let me grow my very own twangy Telecaster family tree, which featured me playing with the likes of James Burton, Vince Gill, Albert Lee, John Jorgenson, Brent Mason, Redd Volkaert, and Steve Wariner. If you want to hear who I really am as a guitar player, you can add up all of those amazing musicians and see my roots showing.

> *The album gave me a chance to tip the hat to some of the people whose inspiration has gotten me this far.*

For that reason, it meant the world to me when "Cluster Pluck" won the Grammy for Best Country Instrumental in 2009. Whatever else I may do, I consider it to be one of my crowning achievements that I got to be part of the reason some of our finest guitar players *ever*—James Burton, John Jorgenson, Albert Lee, Brent Mason, and Redd Volkaert—could now call themselves Grammy winners. On the other hand, Vince Gill and Steve Wariner were already Grammy winners, but hey, guys, you're welcome.

Guitar Tips from Brad

LESSON #8

Don't fret those frets. They are your friends.

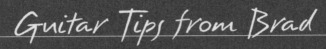

9

THIS IS
COUNTRY MUSIC

It ain't hip to sing about tractors, trucks, little towns, and mama,
yeah that might be true.
But this is country music and we do.

—"This Is Country Music,"
written by Brad Paisley and Chris DuBois

Country music is many things to many people. At its best, country music gives us pictures of our lives as they develop before our eyes.

More than any album I've ever made and maybe ever will make, *American Saturday Night*—released in June 2009—reflected what was going on in the world at that moment and what was happening in my own little world with my family. Our personal world was expanding too. I recorded *American Saturday Night* just as Kim and I were preparing to welcome our second child into this world—Jasper Warren, named in honor of my late grandfather. We took Jasper home, where his big brother Huck couldn't wait to warmly welcome him. And soon enough fight with him as well.

Becoming a parent changes the way you see yourself and the world. I'm not the first to say that, I know. I think it's safe to say that you can see a lot of those changes all over the *American Saturday Night* album. Take the song "Welcome to the Future." When I was writing this song with Chris DuBois, there were really three things I wanted that song to do all at once. The idea was to show you our world today not only through my eyes, but also through the eyes of my grandfather and my young sons—and to serve up a little multigenerational truth with a strong sense of hope and possibility.

Being a dad now, I was well aware that I was making music that my kids may actually hear someday, and I think that awareness hit home in the best way. As a parent, you tend to feel so much more than you have ever felt before. Having a child is to have your heart go walking around without you. Just about the best and most joyful out-of-body experience that I know. On the *American Saturday Night* album, I made a decision not to shy away from writing about everything that I was experiencing, and as a result, the album became a kind of musical autobiography in a way I'd never dared try before. I just decided to let the album be what it would be—whether that meant writing about Kim, about my sons on a song like "Anything Like Me," or just about myself and all the thoughts running around my head at the time.

But to be a parent is also to take the state of the world

a little more seriously, and *American Saturday Night* was also written in the midst of a presidential election, so I had to take a longer look at the whole world through a new set of eyes. Frankly, I don't really care if you're a Republican, a Democrat, Tea Party, Sausage Party, or whatever party knocks you out, but I think we can all take just a moment to be amazed at the remarkable changes all around us.

My grandfather went to the Philippines during World War II to fight the Japanese, and now a few generations later I record for Sony Records and have toured twice in Japan. By the same token, a lot of us grew up under the impression that a black man didn't have a chance at becoming president of the United States. As a parent, I'm happy that my kids will no longer think the color of your skin determines who is eligible to hold that high office. So as a very proud American who has been able to live my own version of the American Dream, I was very honored to go to the White House in July 2009 and do my first live performance of "Welcome to the Future" for our president and the

> *I don't really care if you're a Republican, a Democrat, Tea Party, Sausage Party, or whatever party knocks you out, but I think we can all take just a moment to be amazed at the remarkable changes all around us.*

First Lady as part of "A Country Music Celebration." This celebration brought me together with Alison Krauss and with my first famous fan, Charley Pride, who'd made a point of cheering me on back when I was a kid at the Wheeling Jamboree.

And now, a few short years later, the same kid who was given a Sears Silvertone guitar on his eighth Christmas had written and recorded his way to performing at 1600 Pennsylvania Avenue. I know of no other Christmas gift that could possibly contain this much potential to shape a life.

In retrospect, *American Saturday Night* feels like a unique album for me. As I write these words, I am readying my next record, *This Is Country Music*. The album feels like a very different chapter, less personal, more rootsy. *This Is Country Music* isn't really about any large issues or even necessarily about me. Just the other night, I realized that a lot of my songs on the *ASN* album start with the word "I." Not the new record—for some reason, a lot of the new songs begin with words like "she," or "you're," or "he." If there's a thread to *This Is Country Music*, then it's about storytelling and looking at life from a perspective bigger than my own.

Speaking of bigger, the tours I was taking to bring all these musical stories to the people got larger and larger as I hit the road in the wake of *American Saturday Night*. But as we prepared to launch my biggest show yet, the H20 Tour—named in honor of my single "Water"—we had no idea what was about to happen.

ꟼ ⊙ ♂ꟼ

Just as we were making final preparations to launch the first leg of the H20 Tour in May 2010, something happened that changed the way I look at touring, and my crew, forever. In the first two days of May, over nineteen inches of rain fell on Nashville, and the Cumberland River rose and crested at more than fifty feet—a level it hadn't reached since 1937. Tragically, there were twenty-one deaths reported in Tennessee, and more souls lost in Mississippi and Kentucky too. The floods displaced thousands in Tennessee and tremendously damaged many of Nashville's most familiar landmarks, including the Opryland Hotel, the Schermerhorn Symphony Center, and the Grand Ole Opry House itself.

In light of all that happened to so many friends and neighbors in Nashville, I'm a little reluctant to mention the impact the flood had on our now ironically named H20 Tour. Yet for the record, here's what happened: a very big mess.

Personally, I lost every single guitar and amp that I tour

with besides my main old paisley Telecaster, which happened to be with me at home that day. All of our equipment was in a storage facility that flooded, so *everything* we had ready to go on the road for the tour was suddenly gone. This included drums, keyboards, speakers, mandolins, risers, and cases. And my entire custom effects rack, which was covered in river mud—somehow the water had found its way into the seams of the case. Also destroyed were my beloved amps—which, as a lifelong amp-head, *really* hurt.

If you take a look at the *Underwater* documentary for GAC, which we started shooting about the tour before the flood hit, you can see for yourself what happened when they opened up my guitar container and all this water just came pouring out. Fortunately, I made a call to my friend Bill Crook at Crook Custom Guitars, who makes my electric guitars just the way I like them—one at a time with a real dedication to vintage craftsmanship—and he got right to work making me some new ones.

And so, in the wake of what some called a thousand-year flood, mounting our H20 Tour suddenly became, without a doubt, one of the bigger professional challenges of our lives for absolutely everyone in our little touring village—and mind you, these tours can be a pretty decent-sized challenge even without a natural disaster. Put it this way: three weeks prior to the tour we had almost everything we needed to start that tour. Then our H20 Tour—celebrating the joy and romance of water in our lives—was suddenly in the middle of a total disaster zone created by too much water.

We now had almost nothing we needed to start that tour. We had no stage because it was set up at the arena and got flooded. We had no guitar amps. We had a video wall that suddenly looked more like a chessboard. The only things working were our lights, because most of them were already hanging on the ceiling and thankfully, the water didn't reach *that* high. Now, it's quite hard to do a big concert without any guitars or a PA system, but rest assured, we were going to be really well lit as we stood there doing absolutely nothing.

Fortunately, my team simply refused to let us do absolutely nothing.

By Monday afternoon, we were already ordering the new gear we desperately needed to get the tour started. I needed cables. I needed guitar effects. Possibly I needed a little therapy, but first I needed new amps, and the folks at Dr. Z Amplification started building me new ones right away in Cleveland, so they could ship them to us in time. Meanwhile, the folks at Moo TV somehow managed to pull together enough video so that our show would still look like a million dollars.

I will always be very proud of and thankful for what every one of them did to move heaven and earth and get our show on the road for us and for our fans too. I can tell you that we didn't sleep very much those few weeks. Everyone pulled together and supported one another. It was an unbelievable thing to watch, because even I didn't know if we were capable of pulling it off. We had to summon up our better angels to achieve this feat. There was no taking anyone for granted because we needed everybody's best efforts, and we got them. We only got all of it together the day before the show. Our team showed the same spirit of cooperation that the town of Nashville showed as everyone reached out to help their neighbors.

The country community also came together to do what we could. But it took the American media a while to understand what a big story this was. I tried to help, and I must admit it was pretty strange to find myself on CNN talking with Anderson Cooper about my conversation with the president of the United States to discuss how Nashville was doing.

Finally, we started our H20 Tour in Virginia Beach, right on schedule. We were joined for the tour by Darius Rucker and Justin Moore on the main stage, and for the first time we also had a second stage in our own Water World Plaza, where we presented Easton Corbin, Steel Magnolia, and Josh Thompson.

That first show was one of the most emotional and triumphant moments I will ever experience onstage. I'm sure the people in the audience that night had no earthly idea what it had taken to bring all this together on time. That didn't matter so much. What mattered is that we knew. My whole team would never be the same.

As I made my big onstage entrance in Virginia Beach that night, I literally came up out of the water and suddenly, there was a whole different sort of waterworks. Thinking about everything we'd all just gone through, and about how lucky I am to have such people in my life, along with my wife and our two healthy and happy boys, I teared up again. I couldn't sing our first song, "Water," until I stopped crying tears of joy.

You win some guitars. You lose some guitars.

Yes, in 2010, I lost a lot of guitars, but when I think back on it, I'm pretty sure what I will remember most about that time is the one guitar I gained. I have always wanted a prewar Martin acoustic guitar, but they can cost hundreds of thousands of dollars, so it definitely seemed like an extravagance for a kid from Glen Dale, West Virginia. But after having lost my entire touring collection, and with a large insurance check in hand, it felt like maybe the guitar angels were trying to tell me something.

So in the wake of this tragedy, I went to Gruhn Guitars in Nashville, a fantastic, one-of-a-kind store where you can walk to the second floor and play ten prewar Martin guitars. As far as I'm concerned, Gruhn's is the best place in the world for a vintage-guitar man like me; very few other stores would have even two herringbone D-28s, but they have a dozen or so hanging there like fruit. So there I was, fantasizing over these amazing works of art. I went through strumming one at a time, really just soaking it in. But when my hands hit one particular guitar, those aforementioned angels sang.

> *Sometimes guitars find their way home like a lost dog.*

In every way, this Martin struck me as the most perfect instrument imaginable. When the right guitar hits your hands, it feels a little like a love connection, and right away I felt strangely and strongly connected to this one. Call it a guitar player's sixth sense. As I was about to discover, sometimes guitars find their way home like a lost dog.

Like a guy with a crush, I found myself going back to the store every few days just to play it and be close to it again and again. Then I asked my favorite guitar whisperer, Joe Glaser, to come with me to look at this Martin and see if it was as good as I thought it was. Joe checked it out, strummed it a few times, and said, "Buy it!" So as I was wrapping my head around actually owning this gem, the Gruhn staff brought out a framed account of the guitar's history written by the daughter of the man who had owned it for most of its long life.

All I knew was that this instrument had come from San Diego. But that wasn't the whole story. The daughter of the man who owned it wrote that back in 1936, her father had been given a beat-up old guitar by his own dad and was told that if he played it to suitable proficiency, then his father would buy him the best guitar he could find. Well, he must have made the grade because in 1938, his father paid a local musician named Cowboy Loye Pack to go to Nazareth, Pennsylvania, and pick up a Martin guitar for his son, and not just any Martin guitar, but a 1938 herringbone Martin D-28. The best guitar money could buy.

Here's the detail that made me realize that I was somehow fated to have this guitar. The woman explained that her grandfather had the money to buy such a good guitar because he had a good job during the Great Depression as a telegrapher for the B & O Railroad in Colfax, West Virginia. I couldn't believe my eyes because that station was literally one station down the line from *my* grandfather's own eventual place of employment, where he did the same exact job: telegrapher for the B & O Railroad.

During World War II, this man enlisted—just like my grandfather—and took the Martin guitar along with him to all sorts of exotic places, including Cuba. After he returned, he and his family eventually moved to San Diego and lived there until he died in 1994. Following his death, the Martin guitar gathered dust for a few years. Eventually, the family couldn't bear the sight of this beautiful instrument just sitting there silently, and they brought it to Gruhn's. Then some collector bought the Martin but traded it in for a cleaner example. See, there's a little X mark on this guitar that the daughter scratched on it when she was a little girl and got spanked for. After I had read all this, I realized, okay, I'm buying this no matter what. I could not bear the thought of letting anyone else get this guitar.

My father later told me that the guitar's original owner and my grandfather must have corresponded with each other and spoken by telegraph quite frequently. Dad also said that knowing my grandfather, the two of them would have talked about his three favorite topics: the railroad, country music, and his family. It struck me that the guitar was something my grandfather took up because of his long hours working on the railroad. Think about it: all that time between trains in a small-town station with no TV and not much communication. So there he was by himself with nothing much to do but pick up a guitar and play to pass the time.

When I bought the guitar, I asked the folks at Gruhn Guitars if they would call the family and just let them know that I was the Martin's new owner. I figured that since they were from West Virginia, they might be happy to hear that it was now in the hands of another player from the area.

S O L O

Brad is one of the nicest guys in the business. He's also a really good guitar player and singer. I'm real proud of the husband and dad that he is too. That shows me the real Brad Paisley.

—RICKY SKAGGS

Anyway, my newly purchased 1938 herringbone Martin D-28 finally got delivered the morning Little Jimmy Dickens and I were among those invited to be at the Grand Ole Opry to see the six-foot-wide circle of wood taken from the original Opry stage at the Ryman reset at the Opry House. It's a piece that Hank Williams, Roy Acuff, and Minnie Pearl all walked on, and it was quickly removed for restoration soon after the Cumberland River rose and flooded the Opry House.

At the last moment, it struck that me my first time playing my new old Martin was to be at this ceremony. Like the circle, this guitar was also a piece of wood that had seen a whole lot of history. But it had never made history. Little Jimmy Dickens and I—an eighty-nine-year-old West Virginian and a thirty-seven-year-old West Virginian—stood on that newly restored historic stage and sang "Will the Circle Be Unbroken" together while I played my new favorite guitar for the first time—itself a seventy-year old West Virginian of sorts.

Like the circle, this guitar was also a piece of wood that had seen a whole lot of history.

The very next night, I was playing Charlotte, North Carolina, when fifteen minutes before I hit the stage, I got a surprising note. The note read: "Here are some photos of your guitar—your 38 Martin. Enjoy it." The note came from a Mr. Nichols, the son of the original owner, who unbeknownst to me lived in Charlotte. Fortunately, the note mentioned where he was sitting in the crowd, so I invited him and his family backstage after the show. I told them that even though I'd only owned this guitar for about forty-eight hours, it was already my favorite. He told me, "Well, Dad would have loved you—and you would have loved Dad." They had not seen the guitar in a while, so I brought it out and played them a few songs while we all teared up.

The son even told me that he used to push the strings to stop his father from playing, just like I did with my grandfather and my sons, Huck and Jasper, do now. Then Mr. Nichols tells me of his father's love for traditional music and how they laid him to rest to a recording of "Life's Railway to Heaven." I just shook my head. Of course they did. That also happens to be the very *first* song I ever played for an audience, that very first performance at the Glen Dale United Methodist church, so many years ago.

When I was starting out, I wanted to be a player, a real player. Nothing more. Then I realized that I wanted to be a songwriter and communicate with the world that way too.

Then you have a couple hits, and all of a sudden it's time to put on some kind of show. So in a sense, that part of the picture came last to me. Being a big showman was not what motivated me.

But being the front man of a band is a blast. There is nothing like bonding with a musical group that weathers the miles and the ups and downs right along beside you. Professionals who every night have your back. And I have the best band that I could ever imagine. Like most of the songs we play, these guys are road tested. Basically, we've kept the same group together since 1999 or 2000. My bandleader, Kendal Marcy, on keyboards, banjo, and mandolin; Ben Sesar on drums; Kenny Lewis on bass; Gary Hooker on guitar; Justin Williamson on fiddle and mandolin; and Randle Currie on steel guitar. They are called the Drama Kings. And they have definitely earned that name. You can imagine that in over a decade of highs and lows, there is a sense of family that is only barely eclipsed by DNA. And we have watched as our lives have changed together. From the status on our Facebook pages, to the houses we could afford, to the vehicles we drive, not much is the same.

These guys have been behind me in clubs where we outnumbered the patrons, all the way to venues larger than some cities.

With the musical and emotional backing of these great musicians, I gradually stepped up and tried to become a real front man and a headlining act. In the beginning, I didn't really know who I was going to be as a performer and entertainer, because I came at all this first as a player and then as a songwriter. Eventually, I sang my songs because they were what I wanted to say. It was never part of my original goal to have ten tractor trailers hauling a bunch of video equipment and a PA down the road. Heck, I didn't even know that was a possibility. But it evolved pretty naturally because as more and more people come to see you, you want to blow them away in new and unexpected ways. Like a family, it just keeps growing and growing—if you're lucky.

Over the years, I eventually figured out how we could use the bigness of the event to add value for our fans—for example, by using the video to make it feel like Alison Krauss is there to sing "Whiskey Lullaby" with me some nights. I came to realize that putting on a big show was all about bringing our music to the people in ways they wouldn't expect to be possible.

On November 10, 2010, I had about as much fun as a man can legally have without negative repercussions. It was the night of the forty-fourth annual Country Music Association Awards, otherwise known as Country Music's Biggest Night. It's a show I've been watching since I was a little kid, because to us Nashville hillbillies, the CMA Awards are like the Grammys and the Oscars all wrapped up into one.

For the past three years, I've had the honor and pleasure of hosting the show along with my friend Carrie Underwood, and I think we've found a really good chemistry. The CMA Awards show is a lot of work—and even more fun—and thankfully it brings me together with a colorful and talented group of characters who've become pals, including the show's current executive producer, Robert Deaton; the longtime executive producer, Walter C. Miller; the director, Paul Miller; and the show's writer, David Wild, whose name you might have noticed on the cover of this book.

David is the sexiest writer alive.

David wrote that last line, actually.

At the forty-fourth annual CMA Awards, everything we all planned somehow worked, and the night felt like another dream come true for me. A week or so before the CMA show, I had decided that I didn't want to play a track from *American Saturday Night* or my new *Hits Alive* collection, but instead would play a brand-new and yet-unrecorded song that I wrote with Chris DuBois called "This Is Country Music." To me, this was a true love song written for the music that changed my life forever and to the millions of people out there who feel exactly the same way about it that I do.

As has become a CMA tradition, we ended the night with our biggest award of all, Entertainer of the Year. It's an honor that has long represented the very highest achievement in country music.

My friend Tim McGraw was set to present it, and he walked up to me backstage right before he went out, holding the envelope, and jokingly said, "Wanna peek?" I said, "No, thanks. I'll wait." And there he went, out there to change a little bit of my history forever.

In accepting the award, I made sure to start with someone else's wise words. "My hero Little Jimmy Dickens has a saying, and that is, 'If you see a turtle on a fence post, it had help getting up there.' And I feel just like a turtle on a fence post at this point."

Next I thanked the people who gave me the greatest job in

the world: "First of all, I want to talk to the fans. It sounds like a cliché when you say thanks to the fans. But the great thing about country music fans is when you say 'fans,' I don't even mean mine. You guys are loyal to everyone in this room. It's the most amazing, loyal fan base in the world."

I stand by those words, and I always will. Then I remembered the man who changed everything for me: "My grandfather—tonight for me is about *him*. This is a man who loved Buck Owens, and he loved Johnny Cash and these people. And he said, 'I want you to learn to play guitar because this is going to get you through lonely times, and you'll never be alone with this.' And I don't think he ever thought that it would draw twenty thousand people. But I think about him tonight."

Standing there onstage in front of so many friends and heroes in my adopted home of Nashville, I thought back to watching this very same show a quarter century earlier in West Virginia sitting with my grandfather.

Unless you know something that I don't, my story is far from over. So how on earth do you end a book that's about your life in the middle?

Maybe by talking about the end of another life. A life that made it all possible.

My great-grandmother Lottie Jarvis died in May of 1987. She was very old, of course, and because of that, her death wasn't the least bit shocking or tragic. She had Alzheimer's and had actually been gone for a while. So the whole family packed up and went to Milton, West Virginia, where most of our family is buried. There is a small funeral home there where my other great-grandma had her funeral, along with a few aunts and uncles and such. I know the place well, unfortunately.

Unless you know something that I don't, my story is far from over. So how on earth do you end a book that's about your life in the middle?

My papaw had been having stomach pains for months, but all the tests he had been going through showed nothing. So he made the trip with us. At the viewing, he could tell I was uncomfortable. Of course I was. I was fourteen or so. So he came up to me at the casket and said, "Let's get out of here." We went down the street and had a Coke at a bar that was open in the afternoon. I'll never forget it.

A week or two later they figured out what the pain in his stomach was. He had pancreatic cancer. Inoperable.

The doctors gave him three months.

At fourteen, I don't think it hit me what that meant. Three months was an eternity. Pretty much all summer. And summer seems like forever to a kid. So I would go down to his house for breakfast in the morning, then leave to play outside, and then go back to visit in the evenings. I would sit and play him songs on the guitar, while he sat in his rocking chair, too weak to hold his head up due to chemo. But his spirit was *never* weak. I remember that summer like it was last summer. He was constantly giving me advice and spouting wisdom. He always did that, but never to this degree. "Don't go to your grave owing anybody anything." "Do unto others as . . ." "Profanity is the unintelligent man's way of expressing himself." "Early to bed, early to rise . . ." And so on. It was like he was transferring his hard drive.

Until the morphine. Which stopped the transfer of information completely. In fact, he told my mom and dad not to bring me to the hospital once they started the drip, because he didn't want me to see him that way. So, unbeknownst to me, when the ambulance came to take him to the hospital for constant care, he thought he wouldn't ever see me again. He was on a stretcher. He had tears in his eyes. I rode down on my bike to say good-bye, like it was just another doctor visit. But he knew otherwise.

I begged and begged over the next two weeks to go see him. So my parents gave in and took me to the hospital. When I went into his room I remember that he looked very small and frail. He weighed about 90 pounds. Before the cancer, he'd been a good 185. Now he looked like a prison camp refugee. Or worse. He was staring blankly at the ceiling. I walked in and said, "Hi, Papaw!" When he heard my voice, he turned away. He wouldn't make eye contact with me. Somewhere deep inside, his pride was running the show, and he did not want me to see him that way. He refused to look in my direction. I kept talking to him, telling him how I was doing, that I'd been practicing, and that Hank and the guys said hi. But it was no use. I went home devastated.

Summer was over.

He died about a week later, exactly three months to the day after his diagnosis. September 9, 1987.

So the whole family packed up and went to Milton, West Virginia. Again.

I was crying harder than I'd ever cried in my life as I stood in front of the casket. And there he lay. Or actually, no, he wasn't there at all. I realized that and slipped out. I went down the street to the same bar where he and I got a Coke the last time. My dad figured out where I'd gone and came and sat with me. We didn't say much. Just sat there with our thoughts and emotions. Dad finally broke the silence.

"He's not really gone, you know. He'll be there every time you play."

He meant that when I did shows or performed for people, Papaw would be looking down from heaven. A front-row seat. I see it differently.

He is there every time I play, yes. In front of thousands in concert, millions on TV, or three people in the living room. Or just me. I carry the legacy of the love of music that only a true aficionado like Warren L. Jarvis could bestow. I take his talent, his passion, with me. To the stage of the Opry, to the podium at the CMA Awards, to 1600 Pennsylvania Avenue, and to my own living room. To the same armchair where I muted his playing as a child and now let mine ring out so freely. Well, right up to the moment when his great-grandchildren reach up and mute those six strings once again.

I am the realization of my grandfather's dream. I am a player.

Guitar Tips from Brad

LESSON #9

They call it *playing*. So have fun.

ACKNOWLEDGMENTS
AND THANK-YOU NOTES

This book has been written as a kind of big thank-you note and an acknowledgment of the key players who made a guitar man out of me.

But David and I would also like to tip our hats to some of the men and women who helped make this book itself a reality. First, thank you to the entire team at Howard Books/ Simon & Schuster, including Jonathan Merkh, Becky Nesbitt, Philis Boultinghouse, and Jessica Wong.

We'd like to thank our virtuoso literary agents—Mel Berger at WME and Sarah Lazin at Sarah Lazin Books; Rob Beckham at WME; Bill Simmons, Larry Fitzgerald, Mark Hartley, and the whole gang at the Fitzgerald Hartley Company; as well as four key players—Darlene Bieber, Kendal

Marcy, and Doug and Sandy Paisley, whose gigs go above and beyond even the job description of "mom" and "dad."

David would also like to thank everyone at the Country Music Association and the CMA Awards production team, especially Robert Deaton and Walter C. Miller, who have given us the perfect excuse to spend a few weeks a year talking to one another and allowing that conversation to now become this book.

Finally, thanks to the Paisley family (Kimberly Williams-Paisley, Huck, and Jasper) and the Wild family (Fran Wild, Andrew Wild, and Alec Wild) for putting up with both of us during this process, and in general.

May these circles too be unbroken.

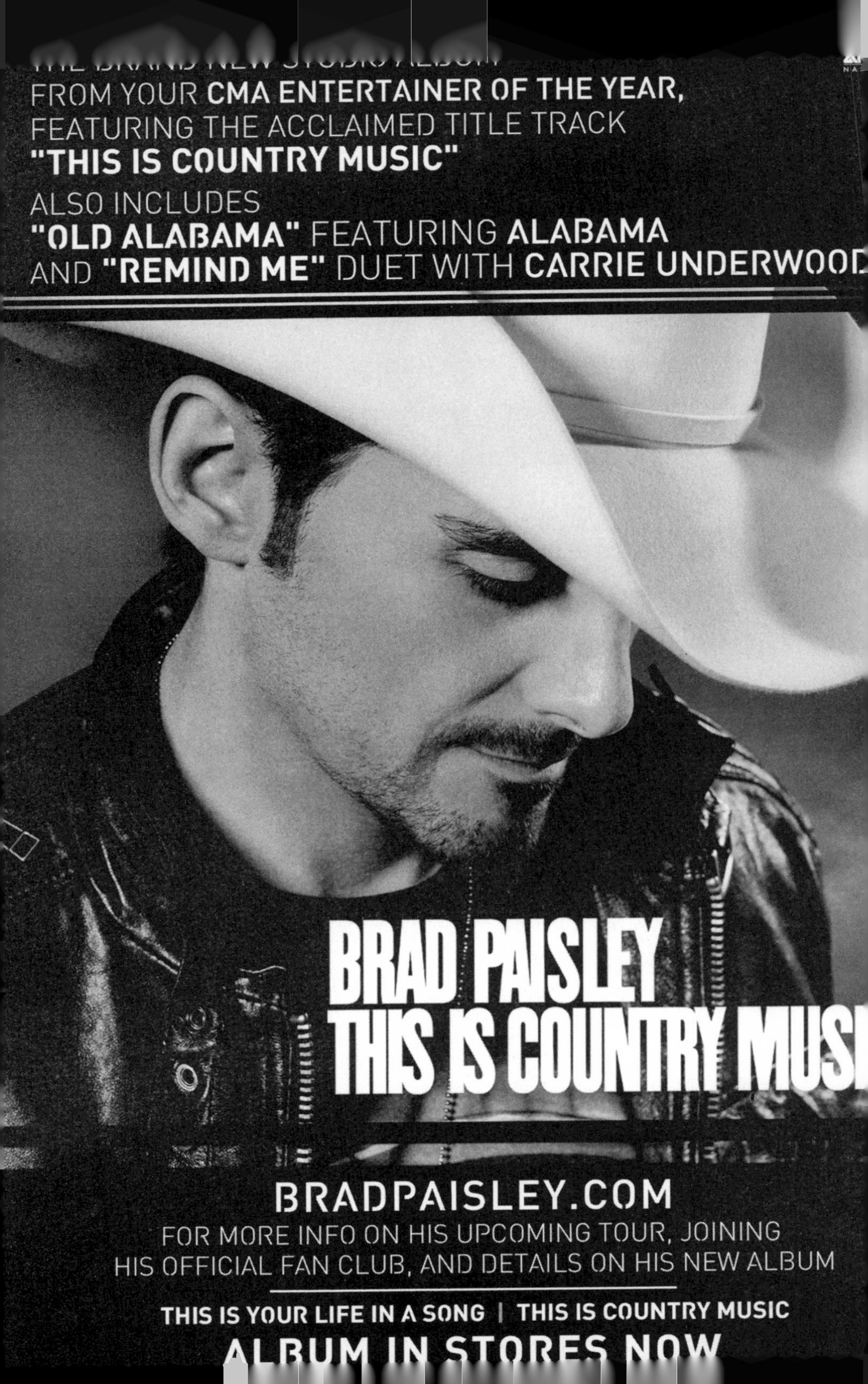
FROM YOUR CMA ENTERTAINER OF THE YEAR,
FEATURING THE ACCLAIMED TITLE TRACK
"THIS IS COUNTRY MUSIC"
ALSO INCLUDES
"OLD ALABAMA" FEATURING ALABAMA
AND "REMIND ME" DUET WITH CARRIE UNDERWOOD
BRAD PAISLEY
THIS IS COUNTRY MUSI
BRADPAISLEY.COM
FOR MORE INFO ON HIS UPCOMING TOUR, JOINING
HIS OFFICIAL FAN CLUB, AND DETAILS ON HIS NEW ALBUM
THIS IS YOUR LIFE IN A SONG | THIS IS COUNTRY MUSIC
ALBUM IN STORES NOW